Still on my way to Hollywood

Still on my way to Hollywood

Ernie Wise

with Trevor Barnes

Duckworth

First published in 1990 by
Gerald Duckworth & Co. Ltd.
The Old Piano Factory
43 Gloucester Crescent, London NW1 7DY

ISBN 0 7156 2338 9

British Library Cataloguing in Publication Data
Wise, Ernie *1925–*
  Still on my way to Hollywood.
  2. Comedy – Biographies
  I. Title   II. Barnes, Trevor *1951–*
  791.092

  ISBN 0–7156–2338–9

Plate acknowledgements

8: D.C. Thompson & Co. Ltd. 10: Associated Newspapers Group. 13:
Newspix, Blackpool. 17, 22, 23, 24, 26: BBC. 20: Joan Williams. 27, 42: PPS.
28, 29, 31, 32, 33, 34, 36: Thames TV. 38: London Daily News.

Photoset in North Wales by
Derek Doyle & Associates, Mold, Clwyd.
Printed in Great Britain by
Redwood Press Ltd, Melksham

Contents

1. An End and a Beginning   9

2. 'Yorkshire Max Miller'   21

3. Song-and-Dance Man   43

4. From Chorus Boy to Cabin Boy   61

5. Splendours and Miseries   81

6. Two of a Kind   113

7. Hurricane in Batley   133

8. Licensed to Amuse   143

9. Six Pennyworth of Wheezes   167

    Index   181

Plates between pages 96 and 97

TO ERIC

the best partner a man could have

1

An End and a Beginning

Success is an inconstant friend and, while it is always welcome, I have learnt to eye it with caution.

In 1971, at the height of its popularity, 'The Morecambe and Wise Show' attracted a television audience of 26 million, found a place in the record books, and won Eric and me a footnote, if not a full-page entry, in the annals of British comedy. We hadn't always been thus honoured.

Twenty years earlier the same Morecambe and Wise had been two second-spot comics at the first house of the Glasgow Empire on a Monday night. We went through our routine in total silence, died a ritual and public death, and came off to the sound of our own footsteps.

'They're beginning to like you,' said the fireman extinguishing a fag-end in a sand bucket as we filed past him, shaking, into the wings.

Such, in essence, have been the far boundary markers of a career that has spanned over half a century. From the moment I took the West End stage by storm as an unknown 13-year-old discovery from Leeds I have been no stranger to fame. No stranger to professional oblivion either; and wide experience has made me familiar with all points in between. For as long as I can remember I have been performing, mentally making my way from Yorkshire to Hollywood, relishing each step along the way, and still not convinced the journey is over.

*

1. An End and a Beginning

Eric's death cut short our partnership in 1984, leaving me not only sad at the loss of a dear friend but full of regret that our professional achievements together were at an end. We had talked of retirement, of course, and in a vague sort of way had resolved to go on just a little longer but to think of packing it all in shortly. If Eric had been alive today we wouldn't still have been performing as a double act. I am convinced of that. At most we would have come together once a year for a Christmas show – but no more. After all, we had been around for a long time and we deserved a rest.

And yet temperamentally I was (and still am) unsuited to resting. Even now I am actively planning a series of non-retirement parties which I hope will be annual events for some years to come. In 1984 the prospect of a pension and slippers was even less appealing. I needed (and still do) the fulfilment that showbusiness provides.

Given that I have been performing since I was six, this is hardly surprising. It is the very air I breathe and I am not good at holding my breath. As things turned out, though, we were spared the dilemma of premature retirement. The decision was made for us in the most painful of ways.

It is the shoes I remember most. Eric's shoes standing marooned and empty on the hotel-room floor when I set off to collect his things after his first heart attack in 1968. Why they affected me as they did I do not know. Was it because they conjured up images of retirement (of hanging them up for good), or that they suggested phrases like 'following in somebody's footsteps' or, worse, 'stepping into dead men's shoes'? I know only that the sight of his shoes, which I called to mind once again when he died, filled me with more sadness than I could have imagined, providing me with yet another incentive to keep working.

This inability to stand still for too long in one place has been the common thread linking my life before my partnership with, and my subsequent career without, Eric. Retirement would never have been for me. I need to be on the move.

It goes without saying that I love to perform – it is the only thing I *can* do – but I love also, if I'm honest, the recognition showbusiness brings. All the fringe compensations which make up for the years of touring, the discomfort of theatrical digs and the sheer hard work.

Driving home one day not long ago, for instance, my wife and I noticed out of the corner of our eye some movement in the car which had pulled up next to ours at the traffic lights. Our yellow Rolls Royce (another fringe compensation) often attracts interest, so we paid no attention. We set off, and at the next set of lights the same scene was repeated. This time Doreen turned and, in some surprise, whispered:

'It's the Princess of Wales. She's smiling at you.'

I looked round and, unable to bow while at the wheel, merely smiled sheepishly. Princess Diana, meanwhile, had produced a sheet of paper on which she began furiously to scribble a message. She held it up, but just as she was about to press it to the glass the lights changed and our cars moved off at unequal speeds, the message transmitted but unreceived. What it said I can only imagine, but it was one of the loftier and more unexpected tributes of a lifetime in showbusiness.

At a lowlier level recognition takes the form of a simple 'hello' and the assumption of a complete stranger that he has the right to greet me as a friend. Driving home again one evening I had an unfortunate encounter with a police car in the fast lane. In fact I hit it. Convinced I was in the right, I tried to argue with the constable.

'No wonder I hit you,' I said. 'You shouldn't have been parked in the fast lane.' (He had stopped a car and was breathalising a motorist.)

'You're not obliged to say anything, sir,' he said solemnly, 'but anything you do say will be taken down and may be used as evidence.' And then, after a short pause, 'By the way, Ernie, can I have your autograph?'

*

Fame has its advantages. It elevates a performer above the crowd but, at the same time, makes him public property. Over the years Eric and I became accustomed to the unself-conscious familiarity generated by our appearance on stage.

Once we were playing the Preston Guildhall, a venue the size of a football stadium, when an old lady stood up at the back and shouted to us, 'Eric, Ernie, could I have a word with you?'

'What, here?' we replied.

'Yes.' And she strolled to the front.

'That's better,' she said, looking up at us on stage, 'I couldn't see you back there and I just wanted to know what you looked like close up.'

Another time we were nearing the end of our act when two ladies in the front row stood up and made their way to the aisle.

'Have we upset you, ladies?' Eric enquired from the stage.

'Oh, no, Eric, we've just got to leave for the last bus home. We've told our friends here to tell us tomorrow what we've missed. Good night.'

It prompted one of the first of our many catchphrases. Eric looked at the audience in mock surprise and said, 'There's no answer to that!' There wasn't. They were gone.

The familiarity people felt they could enjoy with us led them to believe that our routines were easy – that there was nothing to them, that what we were doing was as natural and spontaneous as telling a joke in a pub, making it up as we went along. It led an admirer to send in a script for inclusion in one of our later television shows. Its economy was breathtaking: 'Eric slaps Ernie on the face, puts his arm round him and says "My little fat friend". Then Ernie says "There's no answer to that". Eric then says "You can't see the join", and Ernie replies "What do you think of it so far?" '

This genuine, unsolicited script came complete with a P.S.: 'You can put the rest in yourselves.'

*

But fame can be very demanding. We were constantly on call as after-dinner speakers, but we were wary of accepting such engagements because it doesn't automatically follow that a popular celebrity is a good speech-writer. And if we were tired or busy we might not get the opportunity to deliver an entertaining address.

We used to say we were on a hiding to nothing. If we made a good speech, we got no credit because it was expected of us; if we made a lousy one it lost us fans by the hundreds.

This abiding principle was perfectly and uncomfortably exemplified by the comedian Dick Emery. And we know, because we were there to witness it in all its exquisite embarrassment.

We had been invited to a presentation for the motor trade. Dick had been booked to do the talking and he began with a funny, if rather tasteless, joke about an RAF pilot taken prisoner by the Germans. The pilot was approached by the camp doctor who told him, 'Bad news, I'm afraid. Your injuries made it necessary for us to remove your leg.'

With a shrug of resignation the pilot asked a favour: 'For sentiment's sake, will you drop it over London during your next bombing raid?'

The doctor agreed.

A month later there was more bad news: 'This time it's your other leg.'

The pilot shrugged and asked for another favour: 'Again, for sentiment's sake, will you return it home?'

The doctor agreed.

Much later he appeared once more, telling him, 'Now it's your arm.'

'Will you grant me one more wish?' the pilot said. 'Let that, too, be returned home.'

'I'm afraid I can't,' said the doctor.

'Why not?'

'We suspect you may be trying to escape.'

Now, in retrospect, we may think it was unwise to risk that one in unfamiliar company. But it was doubly unwise when the manager chosen for the award walked up to the platform clearly the owner of a wooden leg himself. He accepted graciously but in a silence not even Dick could fill.

Nor could we help him, because a comedian on his feet is a comedian on his own. What a comic can get away with in a variety theatre in the form of self-contained patter could suddenly become problematical when let loose on the real world. Speeches on formal occasions need only a tiny error of judgment to go disastrously wrong and to lose a performer a good deal of hard-won public admiration.

*

Command Performances were the same. After years of building up a solid body of dependable work we could see its credit diminish at a stroke if we misjudged this prestigious event. We were always caught between two uncomfortable possibilities. Either we could put in a brand new, untried piece of comedy and risk dire failure. Or we could rely on something from our established theatre routine and be assured of a big hit but, thanks to the TV broadcast, risk its becoming so well-known that we couldn't use it a second time on tour. A hiding to nothing yet again!

It is easy for people to look at me and wonder why I am still in love with the business and desperate to stay in it. Isn't success with Morecambe and Wise enough? Why do I need to go on?

The answer is: for the fulfilment. I am a pro and always will be until my face hits the soup. Always on the look-out for new possibilities, I cast an insider's eye on any show I happen to see, in the hope that, if it is suitable, I may find a part.

For instance, I went to New York and saw a fabulous show called 'Anything Goes'. The part of Moonfaced Martin, a sort of comedy priest, struck me as ideal, but after discussion with Tim Rice and my agent it went to the actor Bernard Cribbins. Good luck to him: as for me, I am still on the look-out.

But being independent, as I am, is not always such a good thing. If I am sent lots of scripts and consequently have the opportunity to turn many of them down, I may well turn down the wrong things. Our business is not built for independent people. Performers thrive on a measure of desperation, and an actor is often better when he is hungry for new work than when he is able to reject it as it comes along. Risk brings out the best in all of us, because unpredictability is what showbusiness is really about. We may think we've put on a first-rate perform-ance, but then some little guy comes up to us and says, 'I saw you last night and you were bloody awful.' That little guy is always right. End of argument. Pleasing the public is the beginning and end of it.

*

This is as true today for the rising generation as it was for me when I started out in the Thirties. Mind you, practically everything else has changed! The comic material nowadays, whether in film or television, is far more adult and far nearer the knuckle, but our comedy operated at a much more naive and innocent level. We would have been immediately criticised for doing risqué routines and our audience wouldn't have taken it from us.

It was also, I think, the reason for our success. We were family entertainment: safe, reliable – and still funny. The first time we incorporated a swear-word – and 'bloody' was the furthest we went – we drew a gasp from the audience. This was dangerous territory for us, so we avoided it. That was just our style.

A comedian like Ben Elton, by contrast, revels in that brand of dangerous material and still manages to be extremely funny. The first time I heard his routine I couldn't believe my ears. We have always had blue comics in the business, but to describe Ben Elton I would have to invent a different colour. In anybody else's act the material would have been absolutely filthy.

To be realistic, I think his act *is* absolutely filthy – but he can get away with it because he's good. His brain is razor sharp, his delivery is quite extraordinary and, like him or not, he is original. Not for him a couple of tired gags about Englishmen and Scotsmen.

15

1. An End and a Beginning

When I met Ben Elton by chance at a reception at the BBC I was preparing for a loud chap as brash in reality as he appears on stage. Imagine my surprise, then, when he politely introduced himself to me as an admirer of long standing. Was this charming young lad, whose scripts I couldn't have delivered without blushing, really telling me he had enjoyed our gags with ventriloquists' dummies, or our harmless musical spoofs of Hollywood films? Being more of the Les Dawson than of the Lenny Bruce school, I felt absurdly flattered and rather guilty that I found his material such hard work.

While on the subject, let me offer a few more thoughts on a couple of today's comics.

As a good family entertainer, Russ Abbot is very promising, though I have noticed a worrying tendency in him to use larger and larger props. In comedy it is often the case that the size and number of props are in inverse proportion to the quality of the material, and while Russ Abbot has a sure enough touch I think he needs to be aware of the danger of dwarfing his comedy with too many visual gags.

As for double acts currently doing the rounds, I had expected greater things of Cannon and Ball, who so far haven't lived up to my expectations. Of all those who might have stolen our crown that double act seemed the most likely. Bobby Ball has a wonderful Chaplinesque quality about him which can inspire real sympathy.

Little and Large, on the other hand, are a rather unbalanced act, in my view. I feel the straight man fails to give enough to the partnership, leaving Large, who is talented and strong on impressions, to do all the hard work.

The Two Ronnies were first-class entertainment but not, in essence, a double act as Morecambe and Wise were. I had the feeling that they were two single performers, each with different strengths, who had decided to work together in their shows and then go their separate ways afterwards. Ronnie Barker, the superb comedy actor, and Ronnie Corbett, the accomplished raconteur, were always content to retain their separate identities, whereas our double-act had required our two personalities to become intertwined.

Smith and Jones, of the new wave of comics, fall into a similar category of characters essentially distinct putting on a show together. They are improving all the time and actually developing a closer relationship with each other as time goes on. They are certainly an act to watch.

In a separate category altogether stands David Jason of 'Only Fools and Horses'. He is a consummate performer in an excellent situation comedy which, for my money, is way ahead of the field. Part of the reason I admire him so much is his success in an area Eric and I failed to develop. A really good sit-com written for the two of us would have been a new departure and something which might, I think, have persuaded Eric to carry on in the business with more enthusiasm. No such comedy came our way, however, and I, for once, was left with some regret at the omission.

*

Success in our business is only provisional, and it has to be worked at. Eric always said to me that the reason we were so successful was that we stayed together. A simple enough statement, but also very profound. We were together from 1943, and from that moment on we sweated at it. We were good rehearsers and hard workers who were determined to persevere.

As young lads we did everything together – touring, chasing girls, going to the cinema and, of course, performing. When we got married our private lives diverged, but so hectic was our working life that we saw a lot of each other in the course of any week. We were, I suppose, like brothers who rarely, if ever, quarrelled and could cope with what was an intense partnership without any fear of its overheating.

We had to be careful of mischief-makers early on, people who could put it around that Eric and I did not get on in real life or, when we were married, that our wives hated each other.

Worse, though, were the occasional suggestions that one of us would be better without the other. This was a particular hazard at the outset of our careers when both of us had identities as solo performers with different skills and strengths.

In later years the very notion of either of us going solo again was absurd – as absurd as the suggestion, after Eric's death, that I should team up with someone else. There was only ever one Morecambe and Wise, and once it was made they threw away the mould.

Yet despite the apparent fusion of our single identities into a joint personality we remained very different characters. Eric was nervous: I am calm. Eric couldn't relax, whereas I could go home and shut the door completely on the business if I wanted. He was always sensitive to criticism. He worried if people thought he wasn't funny all the time. He was insecure and needed constant praise to reassure him. I was none of those things. But we balanced one another well enough and, as Eric said, we stayed together for forty-six years. A long time.

Both of us made sacrifices. For the sake of the work Eric was forced to spend long periods away from his home and family. He worried about that and longed to get back to his wife and two children, or to spend a quiet day fishing. Doreen and I always toured together and have therefore avoided the strain of separation, but our sacrifice has been children. When we were married Doreen ran a dancing school – an experience she said was enough to put her off children for life. But the real reason for our decision not to have them was to avoid the problem of constantly being apart from them while we were on tour.

Our professional relationship oscillated constantly between two poles, and oddly enough it ended where it began. At first Eric reluctantly acted the comedy part. He was the funny man with the dopey grin who wore the brim of his hat turned up (these were the days of Max Miller-style comic outfits), while I was rather sophisticated in evening dress and boater (and all of 14 at the time).

There was a part of Eric that longed to be a sort of Cary Grant figure, and part of him that resented being the comic while the straight man had the style. Gradually, though, the act developed along the more conventional lines of comic and feed, and clearly Eric was taking to his role with real flair.

Then again, in later years, our relationship altered quite subtly and we became rather more than just a comedian and a straight man, with an independent though lighter comedy role created especially for me. But it was in the final period of his life that he once more became reluctant to be seen always as the funny man. That was when he had had enough of it all.

It would be a mistake to think of Eric as the classic stereotype – the clown wanting to play Hamlet – but there was a seriousness inside him to which he wanted to give greater expression. His novels, which were well received, allowed him to do this, and he claimed that they had given him greater satisfaction than his comedy work.

But Eric's problem was that although he was growing increasingly weary of his comic role he was relentlessly compelled to act it out. Anywhere he found an audience he began to perform to it despite his stated reluctance. He could never relax. He could never be persuaded to give less than everything in order to amuse. I think he was pulled in two ways. Too tired to go on with conviction and longing for the quiet life, he none the less drove himself to continue and pushed himself further and further until the pressure finally killed him.

The first heart attack was the warning. And, thank God, he heeded it. We cancelled our commitments, took six months off and never again worked at the frantic pace we had so far set ourselves. For six months we knew what normal life was like. We experienced the sheer joy of staying in our homes without constantly thinking about the next variety date in our book. But inexorably the pressure built up again and the second heart attack, when it came, carried with it more than a warning.

Eric made his exit, though, at the height of his powers and in full possession of the two most precious things he could have had: professional respect and public affection. And, of course, when he went, in some ways, half of me went too.

Morecambe and Wise ended for good. That was one story which was complete. But there was life before I met Eric and life after he had gone and now another story was about to begin. It has its origin in a humbler and more innocent era than our own in a time that has long since vanished but whose detail I can call to mind at will. And it begins on the 27th November 1925, not long into another lifelong partnership – that of my parents, Harry and Connie Wiseman. It is here that the running order really starts.

2

'Yorkshire Max Miller'

Our household was as far removed from showbusiness as any household could be. My dad was a railway porter in Leeds and my mum, a highly respectable young lady from Pudsey, worked in a woollen mill where her father was overseer.

Even in the working-class stratum we inhabited there were distinct social divisions. Dad, for instance, was definitely considered to be a notch or two down the scale – a man who had had a hard struggle in life and who came from a poor background even by Leeds standards. When he was 16, two years after his own father had died, he lied about his age and joined the Army, serving in the 1914-18 War where he won a medal for saving a sergeant's life. It was a period about which he was strangely reticent, and he would infuriate me by casually deflecting all the questions I put to him about the war and his part in it.

The attraction between him and Mum was the attraction of opposites, and my railwayman father was clearly thought, in the words of that superannuated old gag, to have married above his station.

Mum was quiet, shy and religious, from a comparatively well-off family which had expected her to do rather better for herself than marry Dad. Indeed, she was eventually cut out of her father's will for going against his wishes and when she left home the only possession she could claim as her own was the piano for which she had saved so hard as a young woman.

I think now of that piano as the focal point of the home

occupying pride of place in the kitchen with the whole family grouped around it singing songs together. I don't think Mum was ever happier than when she was at the keyboard singing 'Jerusalem' or one of the other hymns she had learnt at chapel.

For all that, though, she was temperamentally reluctant to perform in public – the very opposite of my showman father – and so her singing and her playing were destined to go unheard by all except those closest to her.

Between them my parents passed on to me two sets of opposing characteristics which I can still feel working on me simultaneously to this day – the born-to-perform, rather show-off quality of Dad alongside Mum's shyness and quiet introversion.

The single issue which divided them was money. There were endless rows about it. Of course, in common with everyone else, we never seemed to have enough, but the biggest source of tension was not so much that as the chalk-and-cheese attitude each partner had to the everyday realities and demands of the household budget.

Mum was cautious and thrifty, as well she might be with seven mouths to feed on a basic income of two pounds a week. 'Save a little, spend a little and remember that your bank book is your best friend' was one of the constant refrains of my childhood and, if I'm honest, most of my adult life. That caution with money has been one of her lifelong bequests, leaving me with a horror of debt and a steely determination to pay my own way to support the family.

Dad took a more carefree attitude to domestic finance, and although he always tipped up his wages at the end of the week, taking only a tiny portion for a smoke and a drink, he had a reckless way with money which my mother was at a loss to understand.

I always remember him sending off to the newspapers for a 'home cinematograph', an early forerunner of the movie projector, and one day taking delivery of this cheap-jack sort of contraption which he cranked into life to the children's, if not Mother's, great amusement. It came complete with one film which he endlessly projected, in the absence of the screen he was temporarily unable to afford, onto the pantry wall. He never did get round to buying the screen. As a matter of fact he never got round to buying another film either.

This was just the sort of escapade that irritated Mum to the point of fury. What she resented was this waste of money on what she regarded as a totally useless piece of machinery when there were more pressing items like food and clothing to consider. He had the habit of buying all sorts of odds and ends at Woolworth's – tools, toys, bits and pieces which happened to take his fancy – and inevitably, although we kids were delighted with his new and unexpected wheezes, Mother was not.

One exception she made was the radio. That, at least, was a worthwhile purchase which, even at thirty shillings, could be relied on to repay the investment. I vividly recall the day it arrived at our house and the venerated place it was allotted in the kitchen.

Little did I imagine that within four or five years of its arrival I would be appearing on that very radio, courtesy of a local BBC broadcast, in a children's revue. That show, while not one of the world's classic archive recordings, was to be an event of some pride to me and the family and a real talking point in the neighbourhood for weeks. In the meantime, though, my involvement with the medium was confined to making weekly trips to the corner shop where I deposited the spent accumulator before staggering back home with a recharged one without which the wireless was condemned to remain forever mute.

Despite his vaguely eccentric ways Dad was a very practical man, and one of my earliest memories is of him tending a young girl who had been injured in a motorcycle accident outside our house. He was a member of the St John Ambulance at the time, and as soon as he heard the accident he rushed upstairs for his First Aid kit. What I remember is seeing him calmly taking control of the situation and carefully dressing the girl's knee on our kitchen table.

What Mum held against him was his lack of such tangible concern for others in the home. It was all very well, she probably thought, for Dad to go looking after strangers who came a cropper in the street; but what about showing a bit more interest in the family, what about lending more of a hand in the running of the home?

Looking back on it all now, I think he should have been more domesticated. He left Mum with very nearly sole responsibility for bringing up all five of us in a tiny house – first me, the oldest; then Gordon, who went into farming; then Ann, who became a teacher; then Constance, who emigrated to Australia; and finally Arthur, who died of peritonitis at the age of two.

But how could I, as a child, understand his shortcomings? All I saw was this warm, immensely attractive man with a sunny personality and an optimistic disposition, which he has passed on to me. Full of jokes and songs, full of stories and repartee, he would have made the perfect Butlin's Redcoat. His own father had done a bit of singing in the working men's clubs around Leeds, and he seems to have bequeathed that talent to his son.

As a result, by the time I came along, Dad was fairly well established, in a purely amateur sort of way, on the club circuit. In time his solo routine was to develop into a double act when he took on a partner – me – no more than seven years old, and utterly devoted to him.

*

Home, from the age of five, was No. 12, Station Terrace, East Ardsley, between Leeds and Wakefield. We had lived in a couple of houses before that, but this was the place where the details of my early life first became clearly focussed.

It was an end-of-terrace house by an embankment just outside Ardsley Station on the branch line to Bradford: a simple two-up, two-down railway cottage with the front room overlooking the line and the kitchen looking out onto a turnip field.

It had outside lavatories, of course, four in a row, and there was something very special about sitting in there on a cold winter's night singing away – it was advisable to sing as there was never any lock on the door. The *News of the World* was our companion here, its pages torn into neat squares and hanging loosely on a nail now that its primary role had been performed. This was no early attempt at environment-conscious recycling, merely an economic necessity.

At the front of the house there was a shed made out of railway sleepers. It became, in my imagination, a Wild West fort, a log cabin in the mountains, a military outpost in the foothills of the Himalayas where I would play all day long, alternately firing at imaginary marauders and tending the livestock in the cabin compound. When those activities palled, I simply sat quietly within its four walls and took out a comic.

Real life got the better of verisimilitude on one occasion when I attempted a small camp fire on the floor of my Northwest Frontier retreat. The sheets of the trusty *News of the World* took hold alarmingly quickly and soon spread to adjacent parts, threatening to toast pet rabbits and guinea pigs. Although I managed to save them from incineration I could not (nor could my father) put out the flames in time to stop the shed burning down. It was the only time I ever remember him giving me a clip round the ear.

At the back there was a small outhouse containing a copper boiler. Here was enacted that weekly ceremony so common among Northern homes at the time. Monday was washday, when Mum rose at six, heated up the cauldron and set about the sheets and shirts with a 'posser' – a miniature three-legged milking stool on a stick – dunking and pummelling the week's load until it was clean again.

By eight o'clock it was pegged out on the line drying in the breeze. Taking it down, ironing it and putting it all away meant that there was little time to devote to preparing a proper dinner, so on Mondays we had to 'shuffle'. A 'shuffle dinner' was an invention of my mother's. It consisted of what was left over of Sunday's meal plus some mashed potato. 'You'll have to shuffle today' was the ritual announcement signalling that the working week was well and truly underway.

Bathtime on Monday night continued the family ritual. A big tin bath would make its unwelcome appearance in the kitchen, Mum would place it in front of the range and fill it with water from kettles and pans singing away on the iron hob. We took it in turns to wash – all five of us – and if you were last in the queue you knew it. By the time the rest had soaped themselves down with the yellow cake of carbolic the last in line could practically walk on the water.

At about this time my father's mother was living with us. She was blind and occupied the front room of the house. I have never forgotten her puzzling piece of advice to me: 'Remember,' she would tell me solemnly as I peeled a peach for her in her room, 'never to pee in the bath water. If you do it'll give you creepy-crawlies.' Whether I heeded her warning I cannot in all modesty remember, but from the state of the water in the tub at the end of Monday night's bath time I am quite sure that the rest of my brothers and sisters most certainly did not.

The kitchen range dominated the room. It was constantly lit in winter and summer and provided a ready supply of water from two tanks on either side. There was a compartment for baking and hot plates on top for cooking. Mum did a fantastic job of preparing our meals on what I suppose was a pretty primitive piece of equipment. Yorkshire pudding was her speciality, cooked in round tins and served with gravy before a main course, which could be a big bowl of stew with dumplings, followed by a glorious baked rice-pudding.

The kitchen was the room where everything happened. It was here that Mum would darn our socks and patch our trousers, here that she would make rag rugs to cover the bare oilcloth; it was here that Dad would cobble our shoes on his iron last or get out his hair clippers to shave the boys' heads, like coconuts, when our thatch became too unruly. And it was here, in the evening, by the light of the gas mantel, that we would sit and talk and sing.

*

There was no one moment of blinding light when my parents discovered I had the talent to perform. It was a gradual progression from singing hymns at the piano to singing a popular song or two to my mother's accompaniment. When I showed some kind of aptitude for this, Dad decided one day to show me how to tap dance.

'It's easy,' he said. 'All you do is tap your heel down first, then your toe, then your heel, then your toe again … ta-ta-ta-Ta!'

After that preliminary but invaluable instruction I spent every spare moment perfecting the basic step. With or without Mum's accompaniment I was regularly to be seen practising on the oilcloth in the kitchen – ta-ta-ta-Ta, ta-ta-ta-Ta – gradually adding to it two further steps which subsequently became the core of my repertoire. With those three steps I bluffed my way through the clubs and the concert halls of the Leeds amateur and semi-pro circuit, and with those three steps I have been bluffing my way through the business ever since.

It was clear to Dad by now that I had that little something extra which the rest of my brothers and sisters did not and, without actually saying anything, he decided to nurture it. He recruited me as his partner when he performed in the clubs at the week-end.

I should perhaps say a word about his motive for performing. Money. True, there must have been some repressed longing deep down somewhere to be on the stage, but his real reason for doing the rounds was to earn a little extra to supplement the family purse. Two pounds a week did not go far.

It was not, I think, primarily for pleasure that he performed – five days' hard work on the railway left him little spare energy for pleasure as such – but rather out of a vague sense of duty and habit. Originally he had been a signal lamp man, which meant walking the line in all weathers polishing up the lamps on the track. He was never a really fit man, rather thin and consumptive-looking, and this sort of work didn't really agree with him. In fact, he used to blame it for the chronic rheumatism which eventually became arthritis in the last stages of his life.

2. 'Yorkshire Max Miller'

Five days of that sort of work did not automatically make him want to spend the week-end performing in working men's clubs, so he had to force himself for the money's sake. My appearance on the scene, though, as one half of a performing partnership gave him added impetus to go out and entertain and provided him (and me) with wonderful, warm companionship. From that time on I was devoted to Dad, and of all the children I think I was the closest to him.

We would work on our routines in the kitchen. He bought me a pair of clogs and watched me practising the steps on the oilcloth (later I got a wooden tap mat), while he worked on songs by the piano. After a couple of months' rehearsal in the kitchen we were ready for our first appearances on stage under the name of 'Carson and Kid'.

And indeed a kid I certainly was – no more than seven when I first appeared, for money, on a public platform. I loved it. I had found my purpose in life, and from then on the Wild West forts and the mountain stockades faded from my interest to give way to another sort of more permanent imaginative world – show-business.

Of course we didn't have scriptwriters to provide material for us, so we plundered joke books and borrowed (more correctly, stole) gags from comics Dad admired. A standard routine would involve cross-over jokes which, typically, would begin with Dad saying, 'I'm going for a walk.'

To which I would add, 'Oh, so you're going for a fork?'

Dad would then continue with, 'Then I'm going to my uncle's', 'my uncle's' being Northern slang at the time for the pawnbroker's.

'And that's where you're going to pawn the fork' came the tag line.

They were quite appalling gags, really, but they went down well enough, and you could make the cross-over talk stretch for minutes at a time.

Another quite risqué joke we used went: 'There were two fellahs passing by a pub' – it was funny how there were always two fellahs passing by a pub or standing on a street corner, but there we are – 'and one said to the other as he saw a trickle of water coming from under the door, "What's that? White Horse?"

' "No," said the man bending down to taste it. "Fox terrier." '

You have to remember that in a pre-television era audiences weren't as sophisticated as they are today. Mind you, with gags like that we were asking a lot of them by any standards.

*

The clubs we performed at were a step up from pubs, and several rungs down from the Music Hall. They were local Labour and Conservative clubs which provided a drink, a meal and simple entertainment. They would have one large room set aside for the week-end performances with a long bar at one end and a stage at the other. People came in wearing their Sunday best, took a seat at one of those heavy, cast-iron pub tables with the marble tops and were served by waiters in white aprons.

A chairman sat by the side of the stage with a gavel or a bell and would call order just before announcing the next act. There were no microphones, no loudspeakers, nothing between audience and performer. The entertainment conformed to a fairly standard pattern, enlivened by the occasional speciality act, and went more or less as follows:

A soprano might take the stage and knock out a few numbers of the 'We'll Gather Lilacs' variety. Then a comic would appear, followed by a tenor or a baritone. Into this set-up enter 'Carson and Kid', known also at various stages in their career as 'Bert Carson and his Little Wonder' and, named after the local beer, 'The Two Tetleys'.

We used to do a couple of spots each session; each spot lasted about five or six minutes. In the first half there would be the cross-talk and the jokes, which we would follow with light popular songs like 'It Happened on the Beach at Bali-Bali', 'Winter Wonderland', 'I'm Knee-deep in Daisies'.

The pianists in these clubs who used to play this lot from sight were worth their weight in gold. There would be no

2. 'Yorkshire Max Miller'

rehearsal, no 'two-minutes-for-a-run-through'. We merely presented the pianist with our printed song copy, gave him a few rudimentary instructions and off we went.

So we might turn up, say, with a copy of 'Let's Have a Tiddly at the Milk Bar' (this would be 1938 or so when the first Lyons Milk Bars were coming in). We would say, 'Give us a couple of bars introduction. I'll sing the verse. Then I'll go into the chorus, and we'll have the second time bar when we go back to the chorus again for the audience to join in, then back to the verse' ... and so on. The pianists scribbled their notes on the copy and, bingo, we were up there singing:

> Let's have a tiddly at the Milk Bar.
> Let's make a night of it tonight.
> Let's have a tiddly at the Milk Bar.
> Let's paint the town a lovely white.
> You buy a half pint, I'll buy a half pint.
> We'll try to drink a pint somehow.
> Let's have tiddly at the Milk Bar.
> And drink to the dear old cow.

And immediately I would go into a clog dance at high speed. Second spot over!

In those days I used to wear a bowler hat with the brim chopped off, a cut-down evening dress suit, dark jacket and striped trousers, and little red clogs. Other accessories included a Charlie Chaplin-type moustache, a bootlace tie and an enormous comedy safety-pin holding the jacket and trousers together.

Often we did two single spots and a double. That is to say, Dad did his routine, I did mine and in the second half we teamed up into our double act again.

One very successful routine was an Al Jolson number, 'Little Pal'. Dad came on blacked up and wearing a white suit. The tempo would slow down, I would climb up on his knee and the song would begin with Dad singing:

30

Little pal, if daddy goes away.
If some day you should be
On a new daddy's knee
Don't forget about me, little pal.

Then at the end I would sing the refrain back to him:

If some day I should be
On a new daddy's knee
Don't forget about me, little pal.

It was a very sentimental song and it had people weeping in the audience. It may seem hard to imagine someone moved to tears by that, but you have to remember that the 1914-18 War had left emotional wounds which were only just beginning to heal and many people still had memories of their loved ones leaving and going away for good.

The phrase 'sitting on a new daddy's knee', sung with the innocence of a child, had a poignant effect. The sentimentality wasn't bogus. It was a genuine reaction to a popular song which struck a chord with ordinary people. But, more than that, I think, there was simplicity about it which is still the essence of good entertainment. For example, I don't know of many audiences who don't react with real enthusiasm when they hear a good tenor giving a rendition of, say, 'Sorrento'. The principle is the same.

We used to perform three times a week. Once on Saturday evening, once at Sunday dinner time and then again on Sunday evening, and for that we got three pounds and ten shillings – thus doubling Dad's income at a stroke.

We didn't have a car in those days, of course, so transport to and from the clubs was by bus and sometimes by bike. This meant a two-mile walk up 'the Fall' to the main road where we caught a bus to Leeds or Wakefield or wherever we had a date. We knew the timetables by heart, as we did the importance of catching the last bus home, which left at 10 o'clock.

Of course the last bus was always packed tight, and I

remember Dad jostling his way to the front with the cry of 'I'm sorry, I've got a young 'un here and he's got to get home tonight!' Even though the people would scream and shout we always managed to get that bus back.

Once on board I usually fell fast asleep and had to be carried, too exhausted to walk, on my father's shoulder for the last couple of miles to the door. I paid for all this exertion on Monday mornings when I had to be forced unwillingly out of bed and into school.

*

All this activity was, by the way, strictly illegal. I was only seven at the time, and the local education authorities had well-defined rules concerning performances by minors. At seven I should not have been performing at all. Nobody noticed in the early days, but when we became fairly well-known on the circuit inspectors came round and put a stop to it. To get round it we then avoided the areas in which we had been 'spotted' and went further afield where the authorities had not heard of us.

If I had been press-ganged into performing I admit the inspectors would have had a point, but I loved this kind of work and I regarded the authorities' concern as misplaced. Besides, without me, Dad knew he would not have had such a good act. That, in turn, would have meant fewer bookings and, crucially, less money.

So from then on, with Mum and Dad's blessing, we played a game of cat and mouse: if the authorities spotted us in Leeds we moved our activities to Wakefield and if, after a while, they rumbled us in Wakefield we slipped quietly back to Leeds and Bradford. I'm sure in the end they turned a blind eye.

No one had any need to worry about my well-being. The working conditions were far from Dickensian and, being so young, I was always treated with great kindness. In particular on Sundays we would be invited back to people's homes for Sunday dinner – not 'lunch', please note, that came much later.

Without such an invitation Dad and I had to wander round

Leeds at a loose end looking for a restaurant or for somewhere to while away a couple of hours until the evening performance. We avoided that dreary possibility by latching on to someone at the club who invariably suggested we come back with him to share the food his wife had made. I have fond memories of going into strangers' homes as guest of honour, sitting down to huge meals at three o'clock in the afternoon and dozing contentedly on the sofa in front of a roaring fire while Dad chatted away to his new-found friends.

In that way we established a wide network of acquaintances and contacts in the area and could always rely on finding a safe haven in unfamiliar places. It was also good for business – especially if we received an invitation from a club secretary or a similar club official.

*

Our reputation was beginning to spread, and it was rare that we went a week-end without performing somewhere. To get our advance bookings we used to turn up periodically at a club in Holbeck in Leeds where we were expected to do our turn for free. In the audience were the club secretaries from miles around who eyed us much as professional agents might today. At the end of the session we would wave our date-book at them and hope to get it filled for the next three months or so. Even then it was a fairly competitive business.

The performing continued throughout the year and we didn't even take a break for holidays. In the summer the family used to leave for Cleethorpes, a seaside resort on the East coast near Grimsby, and Dad would have ensured beforehand that a couple of club dates had already been lined up. The money we made from these usually paid for the holiday.

Even though by this time I had been performing for three or four years and was therefore something of a seasoned professional, I was still, remember, only 10 years old and at heart just a kid. Many were the times I would be playing happily on the beach only to be told by Dad that I had to leave all that behind to get ready for a club date somewhere nearby. The child in me resented having to interrupt playing with his brothers and sisters in order to go off somewhere into the adult world to sing for his supper, and this early experience taught me very clearly that entertaining is not an easy thing. It's work, hard work.

At Cleethorpes, though, I began to realise it could have useful compensations. Slowly it was dawning on me that all the money we made was handed over to Dad, who in turn passed it on to Mum. I got no reward.

I decided that I was going to employ a little gimmick to ensure what I saw as a fairer distribution of the income. I carefully instructed a couple of my friends to position themselves among the holiday audience in strategic parts of the room and to throw pennies onto the stage while I was performing my high-speed clog dance. This they did and provoked, as I had hopefully anticipated, a similar reaction from the rest of the audience.

Before long pennies were raining onto the stage as I, getting rather cocky by this time, shouted out as I danced: 'Not copper. Silver!' At the end of the performance I had something like two shillings in loose change, which I took home and arranged into a neat pile at the back of the wardrobe. This became my private savings bank, and I know some people who say I still have those same pennies saved even today. They may well be right.

The happiness I felt when I was performing was not balanced by any happiness at school. I was always ill at ease in the classroom, never troublesome but always slightly bored, my thoughts elsewhere. I learnt very little and my memories of schooldays are not good. Thorpe Junior School was a benign enough regime, but Thorpe is overshadowed in my mind by East Ardsley Secondary School, a huge, depressing, Victorian pile where cruel and indifferent teachers stalked the corridors enforcing petty discipline with rods of iron.

One teacher we had was, I remember, a very fine artist, and I admired him for that, but he had the habit of sneaking up on boys if they weren't paying attention and belting them on the temple with his knuckles. As someone who was just plain dumb in class, I was always on the receiving end of his blows and, in more ways than one, his treatment of me left its mark. Needless to say I was constantly being caned as well for inattention. I was not a model pupil.

A more cunning form of psychological cruelty, however, was the speciality of the man we called 'the Toad'. He knew of my interest in showbusiness and knew, too, that outside the school I was earning a bit of a name for myself. He didn't like it, and whenever I found myself in his class he would make some excuse to bring me out to the front.

'Come up here, tap-dancer,' he would say, investing that word with all the sarcasm and disdain he could muster. Whatever he hoped to achieve by such public ridicule I do not know, but its effect was to turn me against the school and all it stood for and to alienate me from my classmates.

Among the many things I have to thank my parents for, their support for me through all this ranks very high. They took my side in everything, and far from considering my interest in showbusiness a matter for shame, as did the Toad, they were immensely proud of me. Throughout the whole of my career they kept a scrapbook of my achievements: cuttings from newspapers describing amateur concert parties in Leeds or Bradford, programmes from youth revues, posters and bill matter – it was all kept. Not only is it an irreplaceable family archive. It is also, more importantly, testimony to the pride they had in their son when others might have turned up their noses.

*

The club dates continued as before, but with a new and welcome feature. We had acquired the use of a car. I should quickly add that it didn't belong to us, we merely had the use of it, but it soon became a source of pride to us both.

One of the few friends I had at school at the time was Eddy Ward – he lived opposite the school itself at No. 41, Bradford Road, above his parents' greengrocer's shop which I can picture

35

vividly even now. We became friends, at least according to Eddy's version of events, after I had saved him from being set on by a couple of lads in the playground. Personally I find such a story impossible to believe as I have never been cast in the heroic mould, but Eddy is sticking to the story so I suppose I should accept it.

Eddy's father, like my own, was pushing his two kids, Eddy and his sister Dorothy, into performing, and they too had an act with which they toured the surrounding clubs. Eddy played the accordion, and later the tenor sax, and Dorothy did a bit of singing and dancing. The three of them travelled, in considerable style, by car.

When Eddy and I became friends we soon realised how much we had in common and suggested that we might join forces. Eddy's dad agreed, and in an atmosphere of warm, boisterous, carefree and unforgettable camaraderie we went to club dates as a fivesome, Dad and I no longer worrying about missing the last bus back home. The sheer joy of those cloudless days lives with me still, and as a result of good companionship and shared experience Eddy and I have remained friends ever since.

*

1936 was an important year for me. From this point I can date my first real launch into mainstream performing. I was 11 years old. For some time the local paper, the *Bradford Telegraph and Argus*, had staged the improbably named 'Nignog Revue'. This was an annual charity event which was put on at the Alhambra Theatre, Bradford and attracted thousands of people during its week-long run. For the rest of the year the Nignogs formed a readers' club for children. Members got a badge and were occasionally invited to talent competitions or charity concert parties where they received pie and peas as a reward for their particular turn.

I soon became a devoted member of the Nignogs and looked forward to any opportunity to perform for them. The Nignog Revue, though, was the highlight of the year, attracting considerable coverage in the local press. 'NIGNOGS WIN AGAIN', 'BEST EVER SHOW', 'NIGNOGS' GREAT TRIUMPH' – these are just some of the headlines of the time. It was all terribly exciting.

The Nignog Review was run by one Mr Timperley, an employee of the *Telegraph and Argus*, I think, and a man absolutely devoted to staging first-class children's entertainment. He put together sketches and scenes and songs in a revue format that stood comparison with a lot of professional performances. The Nignogs acted as a magnet, attracting junior talent from miles around.

At the beginning I was not the principal comedian, but I was given a speciality act to perform. I sang 'The Lambeth Walk' and came on stage leading a Shetland pony. On another occasion I dressed as a girl and sang 'A Little Bit Independent'. Goodness knows who dreamt all this up – Mr Timperley, I suppose – but it went down well.

Joining the Nignogs meant attending rehearsals at regular intervals, all of which I did in addition to the club performances with Dad. My school work suffered even more, but by this stage it was plain where my real affiliations lay. I was never going to be academically-minded; showbusiness in some form or other was clearly going to be my real future.

But there was a problem. Showbusiness for youngsters was acceptable. That was fun, that was OK. But showbusiness as a job for adults was an altogether different proposition, associated with strolling players and loose habits. In short it was frowned on. My future was already mapped out for me. I was to follow Dad onto the railway and become a driver. I would start out as a fireman, shovelling coal into the engine, and gradually make my way up the promotion ladder to the enviable position of train driver. Drivers earned respect and plenty of money. That was the life for me. No question of it. The railway was the proper job, the performing was something I could do in my spare time.

Mum stressed that to me constantly. She ignored me when I protested that the railway was no place for me – not for someone who wanted to be in 'the show business'. Eventually even she began to realise that performing was taking over from everything else in my life. Though she never admitted it publicly, I think she knew that her battle to get me onto the railway was lost before it had properly begun.

I believe Dad felt that way, too, and had done, perhaps secretly, for a long time. These were days of the child performers, the Mickey Rooneys, the Shirley Temples, and I think he had aspirations to transform me into one of those Hollywood stars. I think he found his own life quite humdrum in comparison and looked to the films to get him out of himself. He wanted that for me, too. He was constantly pushing me to audition for this or that.

On one occasion, when we were travelling to a club date by train, he overheard a couple of professionals in the next compartment. Without a moment's hesitation he went along, told them I was a budding performer and asked if they could get me into the professional theatre somehow. I remember giving them an impromptu audition there and then in the railway compartment – rather barefaced cheek, perhaps, but a measure of how keen Dad was to get me on stage and a measure, too, I believe, of how he projected his own ambitions onto me.

*

I was in three Nignog revues in all, from '36 to '38, when I hit the big time in the most dramatic way imaginable.

In the autumn of 1938 the impresario Bryan Michie was touring the North looking for talent for a juvenile revue. We heard he was holding auditions at the Leeds Empire, so Dad duly sent me along. I remember the circumstances very clearly. I did a few jokes, sang a couple of verses of one of my, by now, many standard songs, 'Knee-Deep in Daisies':

I'm knee deep in daisies,
Head over heels in love.
Though I'm acting like a clown

2. 'Yorkshire Max Miller'

In this little one-horse town
I'm lazy, I'm crazy,
Knee-deep in daisies,
Head over heels in love.

and rounded this off with my usual quick-tempo clog dance.

We heard nothing for months afterwards. Hardly surprising, I hear the cynical say. In the meantime life went on much as before: club work with Dad, talent competitions and rehearsals for the Nignogs. I even managed to break into radio when the BBC in Leeds broadcast a showcase programme for local talent. I cracked a couple of jokes, sang 'Let's Have a Tiddly at the Milk Bar' and got paid two guineas. I still have the original contract framed at home.

The radio appearance was greeted with admiration by my family and friends, and although it lent a sort of legitimacy to the glitter of my showbiz performing, significantly increasing my status, it was as nothing compared to the surprise which awaited me in December of that year.

After the months of silence following my audition with Bryan Michie a letter arrived from London. It was from fellow impresario and bandleader Jack Hylton, whose show 'Band Waggon' was on at the Princes Theatre, now the Shaftesbury, in the West End. Tipped off by Bryan Michie, Jack Hylton invited me down to London for an audition. There was great excitement in the house.

I travelled down on the train with Dad on Friday January 7th and gave my audition to Jack Hylton in his office above the theatre. He must have liked me, because that same evening he put me in the show – an unknown 13-year-old sharing the stage in a West End show with Arthur Askey top-of-the-bill. The story made front page news. 'FAME IN A NIGHT FOR 13 YEAR OLD MAX MILLER', 'COMEDIAN, 13, HAILED AS GREAT DISCOVERY', 'RAILWAY PORTER'S SON STAR OVERNIGHT' – I remember the headlines by heart.

Then there were the write-ups:

2. 'Yorkshire Max Miller'

One quarter Max Miller, one quarter Sydney Howard, and the other half a mixture of all the comics who ever amused you – wears a squashed-in billycock hat, striped black and grey city trousers (too small for him), a black frock coat with a pink carnation in the buttonhole, grey spats and brown clogs. His timing and confidence are remarkable. At thirteen he is an old-time performer.

or

He came on without a sign of nerves, full of Yorkshire cockiness, sang – in a voice that made microphones unnecessary, 'I'm Knee-deep in Daisies' and 'Let's Have a Tiddly at the Milk Bar', cracked a pair of North Country jokes, and did a whirlwind stepdance with terrific aplomb and efficiency. He is a sort of Yorkshire Max Miller, tilts his battered bowler over one arm and has a wicked wink.

*

Dad was in the audience that night while I did my single spot – a musical number which I have long since forgotten in all the excitement. How I managed, I don't know. All I had was a piano part which Jack Hylton passed on to the musical director. Then I was up on stage singing in front of a full-piece orchestra – with no time for nerves. One minute I was giving an audition, the next minute I was singing at the footlights. The whole evening passed in a blur of delight and intoxication. When Dad came backstage afterwards there were tears in his eyes.

After the exhilaration came the time for decisions. Jack Hylton, who wanted to engage me there and then, asked Dad to sign a three-year contract. He agreed. And so at the age of 13 I was booked professionally for a West End run earning six pounds a week. Three times my father's weekly wage.

Dad was also offered a contract, but accepting it was never really going to be a possibility. He had a steady job and a family to support so going off into the blue, into the

unpredictable world of showbusiness, was a totally impracti-
cal thing to do. Personally I think he should have accepted,
because Jack Hylton would have looked after him. None the
less he decided against it and returned home after a week, a
sadder man.

Much later Mum told me that going back without me was
the breaking of him. I was the closest to him, I had been his
constant partner and now that I had disappeared from the
scene he had no heart to go on performing. He tried to bring on
the other kids a bit, but they never showed the same aptitude
as I had and in the end he gave up trying. Mum said his
health started to go downhill after that, and with three
pounds a week coming in from me (I always sent home half my
wage) he virtually stopped working. He had stayed on for that
one week to satisfy himself that I was going to be looked after
well and then, heartbroken, he boarded the train back to East
Ardsley alone and, in some ways, abandoned.

Of course, I was unaware of his feelings at the time and
with all the ignorance and insouciance of the 13-year-old that
I was I took to the new life as a duck to water. From that time
on I never lived at home again and I have been travelling and
working in the business ever since – still, in my own mind,
trying to make it to Hollywood.

3

Song-and-Dance Man

For someone who had never travelled further afield than Leeds, London was full of surprises. The first was the hotel where Dad and I were initially booked. It was called, I think, the Shaftesbury, and seemed so ridiculously opulent that I could barely believe we were actually staying there.

It boasted a courtesy light in the loo. Close the door and the light went on, open it and it went off. I remember eyeing this bizarre contraption as a monkey would a clock, and then running to Dad to tell him of my discovery. As a pair of backwoodsmen from the North Country we were constantly impressed by the sophistication of metropolitan life – whether it took the form of the bright lights of a West End show or the flashing light of an automatic lavatory.

When Dad left I was put in the care of Mrs Rodway who became a sort of foster-mother to me. She was hired by Jack Hylton as a showbusiness nanny and chaperone charged specifically with looking after the youngsters in the show. At that time there were three of us: myself, Maureen Potter, who is now a big star in Ireland, and Maureen Flanagan.

By now I had moved from the hotel and was quartered in a small room above an Italian restaurant just off Trafalgar Square. Unused to such exotic cuisine I ate very little and, though I was happy enough to be earning a living as a performer, I was also a little homesick. It was my turn now to go through what Dad had gone through a fortnight earlier. We had been inseparable partners, after all, but success had decreed that we each go our separate and unequal ways. What we had both secretly longed for had actually come true, and now that we had the prize within our grasp we both secretly wished it away.

That, at least, is how I viewed things at the time. Equally, with time, the sadness lifted and I began to settle down into my new life.

Between them Mrs Rodway and Jack Hylton looked after me in every way. Mrs Rodway dealt with the finances, sending half my wage back home, paying for food and rent, giving me a modest amount for pocket money, and banking the rest. I kept charge of the bank book.

Jack Hylton dealt with the professional side of things, of course, but he always allowed himself space to keep a paternal eye on me as well. In fact he took me under his wing and became a surrogate father to me from day one. He saw for example that the Italian food was not entirely suited to my East Ardsley taste, so he regularly invited me into his office to share meals with him.

After rehearsals I would get a message, 'Mr Hylton wants to see you.' I would go upstairs, knock shyly at the door and be welcomed in to share the big pork pie he had sent down to him from Bolton every week. At other times he would be sitting opposite a huge plate of cold tripe which he invited me to attack with vinegar and salt.

He was a very generous man, often handing out sixpences and half crowns to me. On one unforgettable occasion in his office he gave me a ten-shilling note.

The circumstances of that extraordinary event are as clear to me now as they were then. We had just finished our pie and it was time for him to get back down to business. He pulled from his pocket rolls and rolls of banknotes – he had obviously just been paid in cash for something. On to the desk fell hundreds and hundreds of pounds which he began to count methodically. All of a sudden he came across a ten-shilling note which he handed over to me with an encouraging smile. I had never had a ten-bob note before and couldn't believe my luck.

3. Song-and-Dance Man

I think he had a distant affinity with me and saw in me part of the child he, too, had once been. He was a down-to-earth Lancashire man, born in Bolton, who in his earlier days had played the piano in pubs for a living. One day, much later when we were on tour in Newcastle, he glanced at me and reckoned my clothes were not up to much. Immediately he summoned one of his staff, bundled me in the car and had me taken off to one of the big stores where I was kitted out from head to toe in a brand new outfit – from overcoat to underpants, the lot!

Aside from that genuine paternal concern, he also had a shrewd professional eye. He realised that I was a useful, potentially bankable addition to the show. His 'Band Waggon' with Arthur Askey was not doing such good business at the time and he and his associates had decided to inject a bit of new life into it. Hiring an unknown juvenile – and making the front pages with splash headlines – was a publicity coup designed to breathe second wind into a flagging show. Up to a point, I think, the gimmick worked and credit for that goes to him, not to me. In the end, though, it wasn't enough to save the show.

It was Jack Hylton who shaped my stage persona. For a start he changed my name. No longer would I be Ernest Wiseman but, henceforth, Ernie Wise. He knocked the raw edges off my act by taking me out of clogs and putting me into tap shoes. He replaced my battered bowler with a straw hat and put me in a smart dinner suit. Altogether a more sophisticated, slightly up-market image – more Maurice Chevalier than Max Miller now.

Sure, I did the comedy numbers, the gags and the cross-talk, but I was being groomed into the ways of the 'boulevardier'. To put it more simply I was a straightforward song-and-dance man – which is what I still regard myself as to this day.

*

A by-product of this early grooming was the temporary acquisition of fancy ways and grand ideas which, thankfully, have long since disappeared. I had seen Arthur Askey coming out by the stage door, for example, and had watched him signing autographs for the fans outside. One evening, clearly in a hurry, he dashed out into the street, brushed past the waiting crowd with a casual 'Sorry, I haven't got time for autographs' and was gone.

This struck me as incredibly urbane and attractive – the busy, London star racing off to an important assignation in the capital. I determined to copy him.

The next night I calculated my exit into the adoring crowd with near-military precision and with a great show of urgency ran out declaring, 'Sorry, I'm in a rush – I haven't got time for autographs.'

I didn't realise until a moment later that nobody in this 'adoring' throng was remotely interested in me, a cocky little 13-year-old now standing baffled on the pavement opposite and clearly lacking any destination warranting such urgent haste. I never pulled that stunt again.

*

'Band Waggon' at the Princes folded after a few months and Jack Hylton's band went on tour. During this period I was learning all I could from the rest of the cast and adapting the material, thanks to Jack Hylton, to suit changing demand. My songs had more polish: 'Nice People with Nice Manners', 'Run Rabbit Run', that sort of thing.

The Nignog Revues and the club work had laid the foundations. My new experiences in the professional world were now building on them – reshaping my act all the time. According to an early newspaper review I was 'a born artist'. A bit of an exaggeration, that, but it goes on:

> That tilt of the bowler and clever play with the eyes, the genius of Ernest dims not. He has the confidence of the old stager and the delicious naivety of the mere boy. It is all worthy of a Chaplin. Put Ernest in baggy checks or in the pearl embroidered togs of the coster walking Lambeth way and he will still be equal to his job.

Well, all that was beginning to fade away into the past by now. I was being paraded as an altogether slicker product: in many ways an adult before his time, a child without a childhood.

I noticed this at the schools I attended on tour. I was always an outsider with very little in common with my fellow classmates. I was required by law to attend school – a different one for each new venue we performed at – and inevitably I was viewed with suspicion by staff and pupils alike. To be met at four o'clock, however, by Jack Hylton's chauffeur-driven Buick with its white-walled tyres speeding me off to rehearsals did little to help the process of integration.

On the occasions I did mix with my peers I noticed a strange phenomenon. Contrary to what one might have expected I found they were far more worldly-wise than I was. Their knowledge of sex, of smoking, of swearing and so on left me completely puzzled and made me feel like a very much younger brother learning the facts of life from his elders.

The reason for this bizarre reversal of roles I worked out much later. Although I was being brought up among adults, everyone surrounding me was determined to protect me – with the result that I led a very confined life, sheltered from ordinary boyhood influences and rigorously shielded by adults themselves from the raw adult world outside the theatre.

For instance, whenever we moved theatres I would travel with Jack Hylton in his car while the others took a train to the next venue. With the help of Mrs Rodway we juveniles always got to bed relatively early and were assured of a good night's sleep. It was all very proper. The Local Education Authorities had to be forewarned of our arrival, and a representative attended every performance to ensure that the minors were out of the theatre by ten o'clock sharp. If we were a minute late we weren't allowed to go on stage the following night.

It was the very opposite of a deprived childhood. True, I was no longer living at home, but other children from more elevated backgrounds soon got used to this sort of life at public school so why shouldn't I? The theatre was my Eton and Harrow, showbusiness my University of Life. And I was learning all the time.

This wasn't learning in the conventional way, I admit. I do have a residual feeling of regret that I did not study more in my schooldays. I would like to have mastered a language, for instance, or perfected my spelling – a great disadvantage – but I was a lazy learner, prepared to do only those things I instinctively liked doing.

My real regret, though, is never having learnt to play the piano properly. If only I had had the perseverance and Mum had kept me at it I might have turned into something more than the purely instinctive musician I am. Eric was similar to me in that respect and I said to him more than once, 'What we lack in education we've got to make up for with animal cunning.'

*

I first met Eric in the spring of 1939. I was on tour with Jack Hylton, doing a concert at a cinema in Manchester, and all of five months in the business. As was usual, there were open auditions to catch any fleeting talent in the area. It was my usual practice on these occasions to sit out front casting an 'experienced' eye over the ever-hopeful acts. At this point enter Eric Bartholomew accompanied by his mother, the redoubtable Sadie.

Eric took the stage and went into a number called 'I'm not All There'. This he followed with a very polished impression of Flanagan and Allan. How the hell he did it I don't know! He played each character separately but somehow wove them together in such a way that we were convinced there were two people up there on stage. Everybody was terribly impressed – so much so that the boys in the band turned round to me and said (only half-joking!), 'Bye, then, Ernie. Things won't be the same with this new lad around, but I dare say we'll soon get used to him. What are you going to do now?'

48

3. Song-and-Dance Man

I can see him up there to this day. He had on a beret, a cut-down evening suit held together, exactly as I used to have, by a large comedy safety-pin. A strand of hair looped from under the beret in a kiss-curl that came to rest just above his glasses. He wore a gormless, dopey sort of expression as he sucked a huge red lollipop and sang, 'I'm not all there, there's something missing.'

Now, that was funny enough, but the Flanagan and Allan brought gasps of admiration and I began to get seriously worried about my future career. I had a lot of push in those days, a hard core, but I have to admit my self-esteem took a bit of a knock from Eric even though we never said a word to each other. It was another six months before we met again, in Swansea, in a touring production of a juvenile discoveries show entitled 'Youth Takes a Bow'.

In the meantime Jack Hylton's band toured a bit more until, in September, war broke out and all the theatres closed. As all the musicians began to get their call-up papers he was forced to dismantle the band and the show folded for good.

At that point I could have gone back home, but Jack Hylton suggested I come with him to Sussex, to the Villa Daheim, his country house in Angmering-on-Sea on the South coast between the holiday resorts of Bognor Regis and Worthing. For a young lad from East Ardsley it could have been Hawaii. Come to think of it, it was Hawaii!

Such luxury I had never seen before. He and his wife had a chauffeur, a German cook, a German maid and a nanny. I was looked after as one of the family and, even though I wasn't earning a cent for him, I was given pocket money and meals and sweets and lived, in short, high off the hog for months.

I think the family unofficially adopted me. Certainly my invitation to stay was open-ended. But after a while I got homesick again and wanted to see Mum and Dad. Apart from the odd visits they had made to theatres to see me while I was on tour I hadn't had any real contact with them since I had hit the West End all those months ago. So I packed my bags and, with Jack Hylton's blessing, made my way North.

49

3. Song-and-Dance Man

I arrived, unannounced, in the kitchen of No. 17, Oxley Street, Pontefract Lane, Leeds. My parents by this time had moved. Dad was sitting at the table. In retrospect I don't know what I expected – whether bunting and brass bands in the streets outside, or just a smile and a cuddle – but I will never forget the disappointment of that first encounter after so long away from home. My dad turned to me and without registering a flicker of emotion said, 'Why did you come back? You had it made!'

I was immensely sad.

*

Life resumed a near-normal pattern, picking up not quite where it had left off because things had changed. I had changed and, of course, grown older. I was glad to be back home and didn't resent the change of scenery in the slightest. It was a long way from the luxury of Angmering-on-Sea, but I soon settled back into the warmth of long-familiar surroundings.

The one thing I was rather snooty about was the performing. Now that I was a pro I was no longer interested in the local clubs. The magic between Dad and me had vanished forever so we couldn't put on a double act any more and I felt out of place doing a solo spot in venues I felt I had long since left behind. I did do a bit of club work – I had to – to earn money for my keep but I was never happy doing it. I had to do something, though, because I was unemployed. Unemployed at 14. So, for a time, I became a coalman's labourer.

I should have foreseen the problems my arrival back home were bound to cause. I was, after all, just another mouth to feed, and hadn't Mum said often enough to Dad, 'When there's no money in the house, love flies out the window'?

So I got a job with the coalman down the road, helped him bag and deliver his 'nutty slack' and took turns driving the horse and cart down the cobbled streets of suburban Leeds. I earned 17s 6d a week, given to me in the form of seven half-crowns, which was quite a change from the six quid a week I had been used to.

And yet I did not regard this as a come-down in the world at all. You see, although showbusiness is very important to me – more than that, it has been my life – there is one other consideration I hold in equal regard: namely, earning a living. If I can earn my keep, then, however I have to do it, I'm happy. I have never drawn unemployment benefit or sick pay in my life. I have a need to be self-sufficient, independent. My early experiences schooled me in that.

What set me apart from the rest of the kids in the family was that, right from the start, as the elder brother, I was regarded partly as the breadwinner in the household. I always had money and was forever bringing home presents for everyone – food, Easter eggs, sweets, all sorts of things. I have often thought that the epitaph engraved on my tombstone should read, 'R.E.P.: Rest, Ernie the Provider.'

All this is not to say, however, that I took to a coalman's life with relish. I felt I was destined for a wider vista than that of a horse's backside and I was greatly relieved to receive a telegram after a few months from Bryan Michie, inviting me down to Swansea to join a discovery show going under the name of 'Youth Takes a Bow'. The second and decisive phase of my career was about to begin.

*

By the time I arrived at the Swansea Empire I was already something of a child prodigy – a star, albeit in a limited way. I had been written up, with typical newspaper hyperbole, as 'The Jack Buchanan of Tomorrow', 'The Young Max Miller', 'Britain's own Mickey Rooney', and so my arrival among those new discoveries was greeted – so I was told by Eric much later – with reverence. Eric and I soon got chatting and seemed to hit it off straightaway. In those days I was taller than him which is an indication of just how far the two of us go back.

The star of Bryan Michie's discoveries was Mary Naylor, a

pretty girl of about my age, who used to sing 'The Ferryboat Serenade' to her own piano accordion accompaniment. There was also a young harmonica player called Arthur Tolcher, who eventually turned up regularly in our TV series as a successful running gag at the end of the shows. Meanwhile Eric and I did our solo spots. The double act was some way in the future.

After Swansea the show went on tour, doing the rounds of the variety theatres in wartime Britain. By now, of course, I was no longer a delicate flower in need of matrons and chaperones – or, if I was, I wasn't treated as such. Like everyone else, I was expected to make my way from theatre to theatre under my own steam, booking my own digs and making all my travel and other arrangements myself. I was getting about £7 a week at this time, and out of this I had to organise all my expenses. Needless to say, I was still managing to send money back home and to save some into the bargain.

What had begun as a casual friendship with Eric was fused into something like a partnership in Oxford when, on tour, and suddenly arriving in a city thick with British troops, I was unable to find digs. We were playing the New Theatre at the time and I had spent all evening, in the blackout, knocking on landladies' doors and getting polite refusals. Eventually I called at the digs where Eric and his mother were staying, and after a little persuasion the landlady agreed to let me sleep in their room on the floor.

Sadie Bartholomew was really the driving force behind the double act. She was a tiny Lancashire woman, a furious smoker with a tungsten carbide core of solid ambition. She was always encouraging us to team up like the double acts of the day – Moon and Bentley in England and, of course, in America Laurel and Hardy and Abbott and Costello. She was constantly dreaming up new ideas for us, stealing material from other comics for us to incorporate into a routine.

In a supercharged sort of way she was the mirror image of my father who, much earlier, had been the key element in my development. At one point she even bought us a tape-recorder – the biggest contraption I had ever seen – and got us to record our act, play it back and then offer opinions and variations on it, honing it down until we got it right.

I took to her immediately and from then on the three of us were inseparable. We travelled together from engagement to engagement with Sadie taking full control of all the practical arrangements – digs, trains and buses – and as much control as we would let her of our professional act.

The double act started life as a hobby, a sideline which we would work on in addition to the solo spots we each had. We would rehearse in our spare time, put together a short routine and offer it to the show. The big problem   the management was that, if they let us go on with it, somebody else in the show had to come off. That meant two things: first, tears from the luckless young performer selected for the chop, and secondly a stream of complaint, invective and abuse from the theatrical mothers who accompanied their prodigies round the country.

This was far more of a problem for Bryan Michie than a few youthful tears. These women were as tenacious as fox terriers with a bone. They were highly ambitious for their children and, after years on the sidelines of the profession, they knew every dot and comma of the contract. If they didn't get what they felt to be just treatment they could – and did – cause one hell of a lot of trouble for a touring show whose success was always hanging by a thread.

We eventually put together a two-and-a-half minute routine and asked Bryan Michie if he would give it an audition. He agreed and, though he liked what he saw, he made no promises about including it in the show.

For a start there was a problem with the name. No one liked the sound of 'Bartholomew and Wise', so if we were ever going to make it we needed a snappier title. One day in Coventry Sadie was talking to Adelaide Hall, the black singer from America who was appearing much further up on the same bill as we were. As they were discussing the snag with the name, Adelaide's husband, Bert Hicks, came up and told her that a friend of his in America, faced with a similar problem, had taken on the name of his home town, which happened to be Rochester. 'Where was Eric born?' he asked Sadie.

'Morecambe,' she replied. And from that day on the two of us became Morecambe and Wise.

Our routine was pretty raw, but what we lacked in polish we made up for in enthusiasm. The two of us came on together for a quick musical number, a few bars of 'How's about a Little Ramble in the Moonlight', for instance. Then Eric went off and our gags began. He came back on with a fishing rod with an apple on the end to which I said: 'What are you doing?'

'I'm going fishing.'

'But you don't catch fish with an apple. You need a worm.'

'Ah,' said Eric, 'the worm's in the apple.'

Then he would come on with a suitcase.

'What are you doing with that suitcase?' came the feedline.

'I'm taking it to court.'

A few minutes later he would reappear with a ladder and announce:

'I've decided to take it to a higher court.'

It was all terrible stuff, really, but it got the laughs and it went down so well when we were first allowed to try it out at the Liverpool Empire in 1941 that Bryan Michie said we could keep it in the show for the following week.

*

In the meantime we continued with the single acts, pulling the double out of the hat whenever we were given the opportunity. It meant each of us altering his individual stage persona to suit the other's. I, the sophisticated song-and-dance man with the soft shoe shuffle, the blue blazer and the straw hat, had to be prepared to move more into the rough and tumble of comedy, feeding Eric the lines and being ready, if necessary, to be the butt of some of the gags, while Eric had to tone down his gormless 'I'm not All There' routine and refine some of his belly-laugh comedy to suit an altogether slicker product which our double act was slowly becoming.

When I look back at some of our patter in those days, however, I have to say the 'slickness' of the product may have been a piece of wishful thinking on my part. For example:

Eric: I've been in the Army since I was six years old.
Ernie: Impossible. You can't join the Army at six.
Eric: Yes you can. I was in the infantry!

or:

Ernie: You're advancing towards the enemy and suddenly you get an ear shot off. What would you do?
Eric: I'd carry on, sir.
Ernie: You advance a little further and you get the other ear shot off. What then?
Eric: I'd stop.
Ernie: Why?
Eric: I'd have to. The tin hat would be over my eyes!

Terrible stuff, but we kept it in as long as we were getting laughs.

Our models were Abbott and Costello. We even went so far as to deliver some of the material in fake American accents. We pinched our gags from routines we saw them perform in the films and adapted them to suit our needs. When adaptation seemed unnecessary we merely stole.

Stealing, which all the comics did, was sometimes dangerous. One week, I remember, we were appearing with a grizzled old pro in Glasgow and were using material which he considered to be his own. It was material totally unsuited to 14-year-olds, which, of course, is all we were, and involved cross-talk between Eric and me.

I would say, 'My wife's lovely. She was sent to me from Heaven', to which Eric would reply, 'As a punishment, you mean?' It got a big laugh.

When we came off, the comic, red in the face, asked us why we were using his gags. We told him we had got it from so-and-so and asked him if we could go on using it for the week. Reluctantly he agreed.

On the next night we went out, did our spot and included the my-wife-sent-from-Heaven gag. It was received in silence. We continued to use it every night, at a loss to hear it die as soon as we had delivered it. Why, we wondered, if it had gone down well on Monday was it falling flat for the rest of the week? We found out only as the theatre date came to an end. The comic whose nose we had put out of joint was using it every night in the first half.

*

By now our double act was taking up more of our interest than the two singles. As a result the solo acts gradually disappeared and we decided that we stood the best chance of professional survival if we became a partnership. We knew Bryan Michie's 'Discoveries' couldn't last forever, so we had to consider the future.

At 15 we were incapable of planning ahead, of course, but Sadie Bartholomew, true to form, was happy to take all that in hand. She was aware that, even as a 15-year-old, I had a lot of experience of the business behind me and that, having stayed with Jack Hylton at his home, I was extremely well-connected.

Next door to Jack's villa in Angmering-on-Sea lived the great London impresario George Black who was always dropping in to talk business. Although I was then just a kid on the fringes of it all I was being brought up in a professional atmosphere, drinking in all the stage gossip and the wheeling and dealing.

'Why don't you go and see Jack Hylton personally, Ernie,' Sadie used to say to me. 'Go and have a quiet word with George Black. They'll fix you up with something.'

56

This was all in the nature of wishful thinking, however, because, although I knew them well enough, I couldn't expect them suddenly to conjure up a show for our benefit, or even to pull strings on our behalf.

We were still very raw beginners, remember, and it was their view that, at our age, we stood very little chance of making a living in Variety outside the confines of a young discoveries show. We did our best to challenge this notion, but even Sadie reluctantly conceded that we had some way to go before the pair of us could take showbiz by storm.

*

When 'Youth Takes a Bow' eventually came off Eric and I were forced, once again, into temporary unemployment. I travelled over to his home town of Morecambe, and for a while the two of us tried to eke out a living at theatres and concert parties along the coast. But this was wartime, and the sea fronts were like film sets after the day's shooting was over, ghost towns where only the elderly and infirm ventured out of doors. The prospect of two callow entertainers brightening up this particular corner of West Lancashire was remote indeed.

As usual, Sadie was the decisive influence. The only place she felt could offer any opportunity was London so, with faith and optimism out of all proportion to our achievements so far, we set off for the big city once again. We rented a rather cramped flat near Euston station – the opulence of the Shaftesbury Hotel by now a distant memory and its flashing lavatory light a mute recreation of the only strip of neon I was likely to see for some time.

Sadie got us an agent as soon as we arrived and, by a stroke of good luck, we were put forward for some work almost immediately. George Black was holding auditions for 'Strike a New Note', a variety show which seemed tailor-made for our huge and impressive talent!

The two of us went along to the Prince of Wales Theatre, did a seven-minute spot and more or less waited for a liveried flunky to convey the contract to us on a silver plate.

George Black, however, was strangely unenthusiastic. 'How much are you earning these days, boys?' he asked.

And here I learnt my first lesson in financial negotiation the hard way. 'Oh, about twenty pounds between the two of us,' I replied honestly, failing to grasp that elementary principle of pitching the starting rate as high as you dare.

'Right,' he said, 'I'll give you that!'

So we were hired at what our agent told us afterwards was a good £5 below what we could have got.

This was only the first of the disappointments. 'Where do you want us, Mr Black?' we asked enthusiastically, 'First or second half? Do you like the seven minutes or shall we extend the spot?'

We failed to tell him that only by delivering the lines more slowly could we possibly 'extend' the spot. We had no more material. But George Black had ideas of his own.

'Well, I don't want the act at all, boys. But you can join the show doing bits and pieces,' he said.

We were crestfallen. How could he not want us? And what were these 'bits and pieces' he had in mind? With a recklessness bordering on the suicidal I prepared to stand my ground.

'Look here, Mr Black,' I said, pulling myself up to my full height of five foot four inches and staring him unblinkingly in the tie, 'If you don't want our act I'm not at all sure we can accept the offer.'

'Well, what about this proposition, then?' he said, mercifully indulgent at our youthful arrogance. 'Alex Pleon is our second comic. If he ever goes sick you can go on and replace him.'

It seemed a reasonable compromise. Except for one thing. Alex Pleon was a very healthy man. In fact, in the whole history of stand-up comedy I would say that Alex Pleon was its healthiest representative and, short of setting about him with a sock full of billiard balls or waylaying him with a chloroformed towel, there seemed no way of engineering his absence.

3. Song-and-Dance Man

We were in 'Strike a New Note' for over a year and only twice – Heaven knows why – did Alex have to cry off. We thus stepped in at only ten months' notice and did our act in total silence, after each occasion genuinely wishing Alex a speedy recovery.

*

Although we were little more than chorus boys we were gaining invaluable experience. For one thing 'Strike a New Note' was a runaway smash hit and we were picking up on what it was that went into a really polished professional show.

The second thing was that it took us right to the heart of the showbusiness world. Many an evening there would be world-famous names in the audience – Clark Gable, on one occasion, James Stewart, Deborah Kerr, Alfred Hitchcock – who would make a point of coming backstage after the show. All very exciting for a pair of 16-year-olds!

And thirdly, because the 'bits and pieces' we were required to do took very little creative energy we could work on our act in our spare time and still be earning a living. During that wonderful run we even had time to appear on a BBC broadcast in a revue, 'Youth Must Have its Fling', so we were using any and every opportunity to develop our performing.

The show was still running by 27th November 1943, but on that date I moved, in the eyes of His Majesty's Armed Forces, from the juvenile to the adult state and received my call-up papers to help the nation over its temporary crisis.

I left Eric at the Prince of Wales to see out the run and went North to Newcastle where I was convinced that the country, if not the fee-paying public, really did require my services in its hour of need.

LORD JOHN SANGER'S
NEW PRODUCTION
"CIRCUS & VARIETY"
WILL VISIT

BYFLEET RECREATION GROUND

MONDAY APRIL 21

TWO PERFORMANCES AT 4.45 & 7.30

RESERVED CHAIRS 6'- & 4'6. CHILDREN 4'6 & 3'6.
UNRESERVED — 3'6 & 2'-, CHILDREN 2'- & 1'-

BOX OFFICE OPEN FROM 10.0 A.M. ON THE GROUND

BRITAINS GREATEST CLOWN
SPEEDY
DIRECT FROM STARRING IN THE LONDON PANTOMIME DICK WHITTINGTON

LES FLEURETTES
ELECTRICAL FANTASIA
BEAUTIFUL MYSTICAL ILLUSION

OUR LOVELIES
THE FOUR FLASHES
IN DANCING FEET

THE WIZARD OF RHYTHM
SANDERSON
XYLOPHONIST

THE COWBOY & COWGIRL
JOHNNY YELDING
AND
PARTNER IN
WESTERN PASTIMES

EDDIE ROSS
THE BLACK FACED MINSTREL AND HIS BANJO

SPEEDY'S DISCOVERIES
THE STARS OF THE FUTURE

THE
BIG LAUGH
"HORSEY KEEP YOUR TAIL UP"

EVELYNS
DOGS & PIGEONS
THE ACT BEAUTIFUL

THE BROADCASTING FAVOURITE
MOLLIE SEDDON
A THRILL TO YOUR EYES, EARS & HEART

DELIGHTFUL EMMELINE
ON THE
SILVER THREAD
ASSISTED BY SPEEDY

WALTER LUCKEN PRESENTS
PETER
EQUINE MARVEL

THE INTREPID TRAPEZIST

"ENGLANDS MICKEY ROONEY"
ERNIE WISE
THE STAR COMEDIAN OF THE FORCES

ERIC MORECAMBE
IN STRIKE A NEW NOTE IN COMEDY

DO NOT FAIL TO VISIT THE PETS CORNER AFTER THE PERFORMANCE

FOR THE FIRST TIME ON TOUR THE BEST IN CIRCUS, STAGE AND RADIO
IS PRESENTED ON A FULL SIZE STAGE.

4

From Chorus Boy to Cabin Boy

As usual, in this new, costly and international production entitled 'World War II' I failed to get a starring role. I was assigned, courtesy of the Merchant Navy, a walk-on part in the Gas Light and Coke Company, performing the unromantic, important and occasionally hazardous task of bringing coal from Newcastle-upon-Tyne to London where it was unloaded at Battersea Power Station. To be fair, the choice had been mine.

When the call-up papers first arrived I began to panic and immediately contacted the management of 'Strike a New Note' to see if there was any way they could get me out of this tiresome commitment.

While they made ritual noises about 'seeing if we can get you a deferment' nothing came of their efforts. Variety clearly ranked fairly low in the league table of indispensable wartime duties. I was given the choice of the Merchant Navy, the Army or the Mines.

A few months later when Eric's papers arrived he went to the Mines and became a 'Bevin Boy' but I, deciding that the pay in the Merchant Marine looked more attractive, opted for a life at sea. Or so I thought. I little realised that most of my time would be spent in rivers and estuaries or, at most, hugging the English coastline on mind-contracting voyages from North to South and back again.

The French liner the *Compiegne* was to be my home for the next couple of months. On this ship, which I first saw bobbing

61

up and down like a dozing whale on the murky waters of the Tyne, I was to be trained as a steward. 'From showbusiness to this!' I mused, surveying an endlessly mournful scene. I was trained to wait on tables, trained to set tables, trained to clear tables, trained to lift them, shift them, stack them and, probably, if I had stayed long enough, to dance on them as well. I wasn't taught to cook.

My first posting, once trained, was as a cook. I boarded a ship called *The Firelighter* and found myself in charge of the well-being of the engineers. There was a Chief Engineer, a First and Second Engineer and what they called the Donkey Man who did everything the first three couldn't or wouldn't do.

You can imagine what sort of havoc an inexperienced 18-year-old can wreak in the kitchen, or galley as I learnt to call it, when he is first put in charge of a cooking range the size of a small warehouse. After a few days I had mastered the art of preparing soup. Get a bag of bones from somewhere – ask no questions about precisely where – tip them into a saucepan full of water, boil them for a few minutes then add vegetables. Serve, without salt, while the vegetables are still hard and wait for the engineers' compliments.

No compliments came, of course, but nor did complaints. They ate it all without a grumble. The same thing happened when I overcooked the meat and undercooked the potatoes. They ate everything I put before them as if I were a chef on temporary loan from the Ritz. This I took to be a measure of how rough life was going to be at sea. If they could stomach this sort of cooking, I reasoned, what sort of grub had they been getting before?

The food, as things turned out, was the least of their worries. Though the Merchant Navy didn't have the glamorous image of its Royal counterpart, it was suffering fantastic casualties performing its part in the war effort. Ferrying essential supplies to the capital, it was the constant target of air and sea attack, and on my particular run an awful lot of people, especially Tynesiders, lost their lives.

By the time I had joined the worst of it was over, but I still had to take my chances with the rest of the crew steaming down the East Coast along what was known as E-boat alley. The danger was not so much from submarines as from German E-boats and mines, and it wasn't until we were in the Thames Estuary that we could think ourselves safe. And then, of course, we had the return trip to make. I was lucky, though, while at sea, and my only experience of enemy action was confined to the daylight bombings of London which I saw when I was on leave. They were terrifying enough.

*

Shortly after my *Firelighter* posting I was put in what they called 'the pool', a permanent reserve of seamen available for postings anywhere at short notice. One of these involved a period of inactive service on board the fuel tanker the *Ben Reed*. We were delivering aviation fuel to Southampton, loading and unloading the most lethal brew imaginable of inflammable liquids and explosive gases. The thing I remember most is casually unscrewing the fuel tanks and soaking my greasy trousers in them to get them clean – which was probably not, I realise in retrospect, the primary purpose the Ministry of Defence had in mind for the cargo. But there was worse to come.

I was still nominally employed as a cook, but loading and unloading the fuel would mean temporarily curtailing my culinary activity. During these periods no spark or flame was allowed on board for fear of igniting what was in effect a floating bomb. Not well disposed to having to wait until this lengthy operation was complete, I used to take myself off to the bottom of the ship armed with a blowlamp with which I proceeded to heat up the engineers' vegetable and bone soup. This foolhardy and, indeed, criminal action thus ensured that the port of Southampton had more to fear from able seaman Wiseman than it did from the full might of Hitler's forces.

After the *Ben Reed* the coal boats came as something of a

relief. If not inflammable, though, they were awesome in a different sort of way. We worked on them as if in a perpetual, Stygian dust storm. The coal was fed into the hoppers, which in turn fed the dust to all parts of the ship. The grime got into the food, into the beds, into our hair and into our clothes. After a few hours on board we were black from head to foot and our off-duty hours were as uncomfortable as the work.

In such a hostile atmosphere there was no possibility of light relief, and any notion of a song or a dance to cheer up the crew was as incomprehensible as taking tea by a volcano's edge. As a result, my talents were put on ice during a period I regard as the lowest point of my professional life.

*

After a year or so things picked up when I began to realise that being in the pool afforded opportunities regular service didn't. The spells in between postings became longer and longer and I found I was able to contact agents and impresarios with a view to keeping my performing career from fizzling out altogether. I was still a civilian, of course, and had the bare minimum of discipline and supervision, so such moonlighting could easily be squeezed into my rota, giving me the opportunity to go home occasionally, to join a concert here or variety there.

In this semi-employed state I used to telephone Bryan Michie whenever he was touring nearby. He would engage me for a night or a week, or whatever was available, and introduce me as a sort of wartime hero.

'Ladies and gentlemen,' he would say, 'tonight we bring you a boy from the brave Merchant Navy, that fearless convoy bringing supplies of food and fuel to the ports of our land' ... on he would go, milking it for all it was worth ... 'ladies and gentlemen, Ernie Wise.'

Then, on I came, in full naval uniform, singing 'Nice People with Nice Manners' and doing my song-and-dance routine. The uniform was a good draw, and it always meant I went off to rousing applause – the audience totally oblivious of the fact that when not on stage I was singlehandedly threatening to incinerate the country's dockyards or poison essential personnel required for the smooth running of the war effort.

What this experience convinced me of was how little I enjoyed 'ordinary' work and how unsuited to it I had become. Although I am an early riser now, in those days I was rarely out of bed, if I had the choice, before 10 o'clock. I used to say I was 18 before I tasted cornflakes. The Navy life was no life for me.

Like showbusiness, the Navy was a closed world, and seamen, like performers, a breed apart. But there the similarities ended. While pros are, by and large, a gentle lot, some of the guys I met on board ship were as hard as a bag of nails – like pantomime Captain Hooks come to life. I remember one fearsome fight in dry dock in Sunderland. It ended with knives being drawn and just managed, goodness knows how, to stop short of murder.

Then there was their capacity for drink, which was phenomenal. One tough nut in particular had a very simple routine. When the ship docked he would find a bar, stay there until he couldn't stand and return to the ship supported by two friends. He had one suit and one pair of overalls. When he got back on board he would change into the overalls for the rest of the trip and undergo the agony of being without a drink until the next port of call. When the port approached he got out his suit, sponged and pressed it in a ritual fashion and, wearing it with pride, went out on the town until the drink laid him out flat on his back. When he got back on board he would change into the overalls ... etc ... etc.

There were hundreds of guys like him in the Navy, guys who may have spent a year on a tour of duty which could have taken them to the Far East and beyond. They would come back home with a lump sum of four or five hundred pounds – money they hadn't had the opportunity to spend during the voyage – and get rid of it in a week. Drinking away wages in bars only a few hundred yards from the ship was a common occurrence and I think there were very few who actually saw the exotic places they travelled to. Or if they did it was through a semi-permanent alcoholic haze.

*

Not a moment too soon my two years in the Merchant Navy were up, and without any ceremony I went back to civilian life for good. There was no formality. There were no discharge papers – nothing to sign or to take home as a memento. Nobody said, 'That's it. Time's up. You've done your duty. Thank you and goodbye.' There was nothing. I simply drifted away as if the whole experience had never really happened and, once in Civvy Street, set about pulling together the threads of my performing career.

I had more or less decided to abandon the idea of a double act. Somehow it had lost its appeal and I felt happier relying on my existing solo routine for professional survival. By now the paternal hand of Jack Hylton or Bryan Michie was gone, so either way I was on my own.

I wasn't destined to be alone for long, however, because on a trip to London looking for work I happened to bump into Eric and his mother in the centre of town. They were in digs in West London – No. 13, Clifton Gardens, Chiswick, to be precise, owned by a benign and impressive theatrical landlady by the name of Mrs Duer. Sadie suggested I come over and stay with them and, since resisting one of Sadie's 'suggestions' was tantamount to fighting against fate, I found myself once again inextricably bound up with the Bartholomews.

Sadie's dominant personality and straightforward pushiness eventually secured us work with a bizarre travelling outfit revelling in the rather grand title of 'Lord John Sanger's Circus and Variety'. The idea, as the name was intended to suggest, was to combine two distinct forms of entertainment in one. In principle, I suppose, it should have been quite a promising innovation if it brought to audiences the best of both traditions. In practice, though, it turned out to be the lowest common denominator of both and was looked down on by circus and variety people alike. It was neither one thing nor the other.

The centrepiece of this travelling show was the Big Top, a huge off-white marquee capable of enclosing a full-size football pitch and equipped with a stage at one end. With laborious rearrangement of the seating we could transform this basic Variety pattern into something approximating to Circus. It was, to be sure, a pale imitation of a circus ring but, given the nature of the acts we had on the bill, there was no need for anything of Barnum and Bailey proportions.

While bigger outfits could boast lions, tigers and elephants, we had to make do with a more limited menagerie – often little more than semi-domesticated house pets. At our height we had one donkey, one parrot, a couple of hamsters, a team of performing dogs, a ring-tailed lemur and a wallaby. Oh, and bearing in mind the amounts of money we were all earning for this charade, quite a lot of monkeys. Speedy Yelding was our resident clown, a versatile man who was also pressed into service as a tightrope walker, and he, along with Wally Lucken, who ran the dog act, looked after the circus side of things.

Eric and I had been hired as comics for the variety section joining four girl dancers, the singer, Mollie Seddon, and a three-piece band comprising piano, banjo and drums. Even by post-war standards it wasn't a line-up guaranteed to set a town on fire, and to be committed, nightly, to filling up seven hundred seats required an act of faith if not a touch of certifiable lunacy.

Seven hundred seats, of course, needed to be arranged at every venue and seven hundred seats needed to be stored away again before we moved on. We were all expected to share the sweat as well as the glory, so half our time was spent acting as labourers, scene-shifters and general dogsbodies.

Our living conditions didn't provide compensations. While Lord John Sanger travelled in style in a caravan decked out like a Romany gin palace, Eric and I had to share a converted

RAF trailer with the pianist Anton Petrov. He was a very classy, if rather stand-offish, performer who constantly smoked a pipe and filled the one communal space with a perpetual blue haze. A canvas bucket of cold water inside the trailer and a large, stinking canvas-screened pit outside were our only ablutions.

Between us Anton and I looked after the catering arrangements. I had come on a little way since my early days in the Merchant Navy, but the limitations of my skill couldn't be disguised. As a treat we sometimes ate at a hotel or restaurant en route. Anton was despatched in what we called the scout car to place an advance booking.

On a tour through Cornwall during the summer of 1946 he returned to the main body of the party with the promise of cornish pasties, mashed potatoes and peas to be served alfresco at a wayside boarding house up ahead. Places would be laid for all thirty of us and a drop of cider would be provided into the bargain. For once the circus seemed united in simple joy and anticipation of a welcome meal which would put all shared hardship into perspective.

Sadly for us all Anton had forgotten to log his route, and after a series of wrong turnings and retreats the circus had to give up any hope of tasting its cornish pasties and cider. The old lady running the wayside hostelry thus ensured herself a minor footnote in the pages of theatrical history as one of a very few, if not the only one, to be eagerly expecting the arrival of 'Lord John Sanger's Circus and Variety' and disappointed by its failure to appear. She is probably still waiting even now.

Our nightly performances were almost incidental in the six months or so we were on the road. After we had erected the tent we took turns as fairground barkers spieling away in front of the marquee desperately trying to drum up custom. On more than one occasion nobody turned up at all, leaving the pair of us marooned in some godforsaken field wearing full evening dress and Wellington boots.

We once performed to an audience made up of six young

boys, all of them paying half-price. With the cast outnumbering the paying punters we watched in mounting gloom as the six of them made their way to the cheapest seats right at the back and settled in to get their money's worth.

*

At this point I should add that there was one redeeming feature. She was called Doreen Blythe, a 15-year-old from Peterborough, a trained ballet dancer and, by the time I met her, one of the four dancers with John Sanger's Circus. Love at first sight it may have been for me, but it was definitely not for her. We met in Horsham in Surrey before the show got underway, but most of the tour she spent trying to avoid me.

Doreen considered me far too loud and pushy for her taste and, although I have mellowed a lot since then, I have to admit she may have been right at the time. The first moment we met was at an outdoor lunch, sitting at trestle tables surrounded by lavishly painted circus caravans with their bright Edwardian lettering. It was a scene straight out of J.B. Priestley's *Good Companions*. Soup, I remember clearly, was on the menu, and I spent a large part of the time wisecracking about the noise people make when they drink it. Inevitably Doreen made the tiniest slurp, causing Eric and me to break into puerile mirth. Being a very shy girl she became intensely embarrassed, blushed to the core and from then on treated me with a very proper disdain. She told me much later, when we were married, that she was also put off soup for years as a result of this rather insensitive comic caper.

After months of perseverance, though, I gradually began to win her round by toning down my ways and setting in motion a discreet courtship which involved frequent visits to the pictures and the occasional meal at a restaurant. No longer did she and her friend Rose dash into shop doorways when they saw Eric and me approaching. Instead they began to see that there might be something in us after all. But enough of

69

this romantic interlude. There was, you may by now have forgotten, work to be done.

*

Although we were engaged as a variety act it would be truer to say that what we were actually doing was concert party. There is a big difference between the two. While variety consists of, say, an eight-act bill, with each act doing one distinct spot in each half of the show, concert party relies on developing a much more subtle rapport with the audience. It's more a question of talking to people than performing in front of them.

Concert party had its origin in end-of-the-pier shows, seaside entertainment with a soprano, a tenor, a baritone, a pianist, dancers and a light comedian. It was originally Pierrot stuff with powder-white clown costumes, pointed hats and pom-poms. The concert parties always attracted a more genteel audience as opposed to a rougher and readier variety public. They were performed at smaller venues, too, often at the 'posher' end of a seaside town.

Concert party demanded a totally different skill from variety, and for a time Eric and I seriously considered it. We never did get into it, though, mainly, I think, because our particular talent did not quite fit the mould.

Sanger's Circus was very much in the concert-party style, relying as often as it could on that bankable standby, audience participation. A classic routine involved me in nothing simpler than a song that went: 'If I were not upon the stage, a blank-blank I would be.' The 'blank-blank' could be filled with any occupation of our choosing – a window cleaner, an engine driver, a postman – provided it was accompanied by the appropriate actions.

It was a not very sophisticated version of 'Old McDonald Had a Farm' but it could be relied on to get the audience on its feet joining in what was fun for both young old. Variety, by contrast, had its risqué side, the double-entendres, the

70

brashness which made it sometimes unsuitable for children. Concert party was classic family entertainment.

Our own interpretation of it was orchestrated by the circus's musical director – a man who had run a concert party before the war. He had a whole stock of material tried and tested over time which he passed on for us to use. Some of it was pretty homespun stuff, but it got the audience reaction (when there was an audience there in the first place, of course).

One sketch involved Eric and me retiring to bed with a candle. For the first few minutes I did the talking, pretending to have a speech impediment which allowed me to speak only from the right side of my mouth. This usually got a few laughs, since it gave me the opportunity to pull funny faces. Then comes the moment to blow out the candle. I blow, but of course the puff of air comes from the right side and the candle is in front of me. I try again – usually to the mounting laughter of the audience – until I give in.

Then Eric says he will do it for me. As he opens his mouth to speak he reveals his own speech impediment, namely that he can speak only from the left side of his mouth. He blows from the left side and the candle still burns. More laughter. Then we turn our heads so that we are looking each other in the eye, pull another set of facial contortions, blow together and snuff the candle out with our fingers. End of sketch to appreciative applause. It was the kind of gentle gag we could probably not have got away with in variety.

Concert party stood or fell by an artist developing a relationship with an audience, acting as a sort of master of ceremonies throughout the show. Even today I can see the performers who were reared in this tradition. People like Bruce Forsyth, Des O'Connor and Leslie Crowther are the supreme exponents of a skill which needs warmth, personality, gentle teasing humour and a great capacity to ad-lib. They have to perform both to the crowd and with them, spinning out a seamless routine which will involve song, dance, wit and the unpredictable – leaving the safety of the stage to mingle with the audience, for example, reacting to them, leading them on and then, just at the right moment, getting them to join in a musical number while mentally preparing for the finale. In short, thinking on their feet.

Lord John Sanger's Circus and Variety involved us in a lot of this and, though we put on a creditable performance, it was never our forte. For one thing, it is far more suited to a solo performer than to a double act because, while the single performer can concentrate all his attention on a relationship between himself and the public, two performers have to concentrate on their relationship with each other.

Both Eric and I, like anybody else with a bit of experience in the business, could pull ad-libs out of the hat, but we used them to point up our basic interdependence. If the pair of us were to have developed our own individual relationship with the audience our essential cohesion as performers would have suffered and the chemistry between the two of us would have been gravely threatened.

In concert party the line between performer and audience is very slender. The best exponents make you believe there is no line at all as they come down off the stage into your world and, literally or metaphorically, take you back onto the stage into theirs. Our act was different. Our world on stage was complete and enclosed, set apart from the real-life world of the audience in front of us, and the comedy, whether people liked it or not, came from the deliberate and often surreal collision of the two.

*

To get back to the circus, though, where such theorising would have been inconceivable in our raw days just after the war.

At this point in our career we were content merely to have an audience to perform to in the first place. Circus and variety, at least in the precise combination Lord John Sanger's line-up embodied them, were destined to be short-lived.

4. From Chorus Boy to Cabin Boy

The whole enterprise came to a premature end in Nottingham in October 1947 at the celebrated Goose Fair. We had all been summoned into Lord John's caravan some months earlier and told that the only way the show could possibly continue was if we all agreed to a pay cut. My £14 had been cut by half to £7 and, from that moment on, we all knew that the end couldn't be far off.

We pitched the tent in the middle of the fair and hit on the novel, if exhausting, idea of a running cabaret. We danced, joked, and sang non-stop all day long, taking it in turns to collect the money at the booth outside and to drum up custom for our final performance. We dispensed with seats and allowed the public to wander in, stay as long as they wished and wander out again. It was a marathon session which we kept up for three days, each day attracting more than the last.

For a brief moment we all hoped we could rescue the show and breathe fresh life into it. But it was not to be. The show was fatally flawed from the start and despite a magnificent effort from all the cast we couldn't retrieve this doomed endeavour. The Goose Fair was, you might say, a swan song for a turkey, and a few weeks later Eric and I found ourselves back with Mrs Duer in Chiswick – at square one yet again.

*

Square one for a 22-year-old wasn't a pleasant place to be – especially for one whose career had begun in an explosion of promise almost a decade earlier. These were lean times for both of us, when Eric and I had to shed forever our 'discoveries' image and make it into mainstream professional entertainment. During this period we were more often out of work than in it and only thanks to Mrs Duer's generosity did we even manage to retain a roof over our heads.

'Pay me when you're back in funds, boys,' she used to say to us, and in the meantime she let us stay, practically rent-free for weeks.

By this time Sadie had gone back home to Morecambe

leaving the two of us, not before time, to fend for ourselves. We set about looking for work.

If we wanted work we needed an agent. But if we wanted an agent we needed work. The routine went as follows. The two of us, ever hopeful in our early days, would approach an agent, tell him we had an act and wait for the bookings. But no bookings ever came because, as soon as we told the agent we were comics, his first question was, 'Where can I see you perform?'

'Well, we haven't got any dates yet, Mr So-and-So,' we said imploringly, 'that's why we came to see you.'

'Not interested, boys, get yourself a booking. Then maybe I'll come and see you.' It was the archetypal Catch 22 syndrome.

The only way to short-circuit the process was to beg, bribe or cajole the booking manager at one of the theatres into getting us on the bill. We had limited and intermittent success at this, but not enough to convince ourselves that we were really earning a living. Somehow we got by without giving up hope entirely.

Agents are a strange but indispensable fact of life in any artist's career. When he is settled comfortably into a long run of work they are forever on the phone. But the moment he finds himself in a barren patch they become strangely invisible, suddenly called out of the office or constantly 'in a meeting'. By and large, though, we have been very lucky with the agents we have had, especially with Billy Marsh who looked after us until Eric died and who still manages my affairs even now.

Before we had the good fortune to meet Gordon Norval, Frank Pope or Billy Marsh – the only agents we have had – we did encounter one or two disasters. I shall never forget the bogus agent we once ended up with, very early on. Let us call him Mr X.

Mr X had been contacted by a booking manager who had wrongly thought he was our agent. The booking manager offered Mr X a fantastic amount of money – £100 rising to

£120 a week over three years – for the benefit of our services. Mr X then contacted our real agent and, posing as a theatre manager, offered him an equally fantastic sum – £80 rising to £100 per week over three years. We accepted and found out only by accident what he was up to – but not before he had managed to cream off a couple of hundred pounds of our hard-earned cash.

Agents are necessary for an artist's professional survival. Here an apocryphal story will illustrate that fundamental but uneasy dependence. It involves a comedian who comes home to find his wife bound and gagged on the kitchen floor, blood pouring from a deep head wound. All around there is chaos and disorder, the signs of a terrible struggle. Valuables have been stolen and his wife has been brutally beaten.

'What happened?' asks the comic, shocked at the mayhem surrounding him.

'Someone tried to burgle the house. When I tried to stop him he did this to me,' comes the wife's reply.

'Did you get a look at him?'

'Yes, it was your agent.'

'That's terrible,' says the man in disbelief. And then, after a pause, 'Did he leave any dates?'

*

But at this particular point in our career talk of agents is premature. Quite simply, we didn't have one, and acquiring one became a full-time activity in itself. We tried every agent in town, pounding a well-trodden beat from Trafalgar Square to Oxford Street, from Soho to Piccadilly Circus. When we failed to get an audition we tried our second line of attack – a direct appeal to the bookers in the theatres. It was marginally more successful and secured us a couple of dates on the fringes.

Our first real variety spot was at the Palace, Walthamstow, when we were forced to change our names. There was already an act by the name of Campbell and Wise on the bill, so at the last minute we appeared as Morecambe and Wisdom. We went down stupendously badly that night and were secretly glad of the disguise the change of name had afforded us.

Still, we got paid for it and were able to settle some of our debts with the long-suffering Mrs Duer, our guardian angel if ever there was one. The rest of the time we just mooched around growing increasingly alarmed at the prospect of life-long unemployment.

Although we were unaware of it at the time the days of variety were drawing to a close. The heyday of the genre, when the London Palladium attracted the top American performers and when even the smaller provincial theatres were packed to capacity, had been before the war. Although there was still some life in it – thank goodness, or where would we have been? – things had changed for good.

In a misguided attempt to keep variety afloat a lot of managers introduced nude shows, which gave a very short-lived boost to their revenue but succeeded in the long term only in coarsening the nature of the entertainment and driving out forever what vestiges of a family audience there still remained. The nude shows were the death of variety and, very nearly, the death of us.

The idea was that the nudes – all female, of course – should strike classical or artistic poses. Movement was strictly banned by the Lord Chamberlain. If the girls were scantily clad, with feathers and ribbon stuck to strategic parts of their person, they were allowed to parade around a bit, but if the 'artistic' demands of a scene required nudity the girls had to freeze. And if it was draughty, as it inevitably was at most of the joints they played, then 'freeze' they did. It was all very discreet by today's standards, but then it was quite shocking.

The temple to nudity at that time was the Windmill, and its high priest was one Vivian Van Damm – known affectionately or otherwise as VD. VD owned the Windmill Theatre in Great Windmill Street, Soho and turned it into an all-day revue, alternating variety acts with nude girls grouped artistically – always artistically – in exotic tableaux. Many of the great names of British entertainment started their careers at the Windmill and an unlucky few ended them there.

You see, people didn't come to the Windmill primarily for the vaudeville. Or, more correctly, *men* didn't come to the Windmill primarily for the vaudeville. They came for the girls. Entertainers merely 'filled in' between nudes. And since the nudes were the real entertainment, the public took to the 'entertainers' as ducks do to orange sauce.

Such were our fortunes in 1949, however, that Eric and I decided to approach VD and try for an audition. We were shown up to his tiny office one Sunday morning and after we had performed a ten-minute routine he agreed to book us at £25 for one week with a five-week option at the end of it. We started on Monday. We didn't go down well.

We took the stage to complete silence, and the baleful stares of a dozen or so whey-faced men with raincoats on their knees. We greeted them with the usual 'Hello, music lovers' and received the kind of welcome reserved for photographers at funerals. Our few minutes of patter were delivered amid grudging impatience and mute irritation. Then we left the stage as noiselessly as we had taken it, to be succeeded by a chorus line of naked girls who brought the rows of embalmed faces into mysterious and temporary life. Our spot was over. But it was just the beginning. We were booked for six shows a day.

Life didn't get any easier on stage, although it had its distractions off. The girls were very blasé about their work and insisted that we, too, would get used to it after a few weeks. I don't think we ever did – for one thing, we weren't there long enough – and I told Eric that if he didn't blink he would go blind. By Tuesday we were used to the routine and went out expecting no audience reaction at all.

We were never disappointed. The only sign of life out here was the rush of bodies towards a seat near the stage whenever one became vacant.

In time this was dubbed 'The Windmill Steeplechase' as the members of the audience cleared row after row of seats to get

77

a closer view from the front. Others unwilling – or often, for decency's sake, unable – to stand upright and move places continued the racing theme by equipping themselves with binoculars the better to study the form.

By Wednesday we were fired. 'I'm not taking the option up, boys,' said VD with all the charm of a surgeon telling you the worst. 'You'll have to leave at the end of the week.'

An act by the name of 'Hank and Scott' was apparently a better draw, so we were to receive the order of the boot. 'Hank', it turned out, was none other than Tony Hancock, himself starting out in entertainment and clearly making a bigger impact than we were.

*

Such a premature dismissal came as a double blow. Not only was it a shock to our self-esteem but it was also disastrous for our plans to attract an agent. We had calculated that a six-week run would be perfect for us to sharpen up the act and to invite a selection of agents to this showcase venue in the West End. We now had only four days to entice someone along.

Out of our wages we paid for a string of complimentary tickets which we dispatched to agents throughout the city. We also paid for an advertisement in *The Stage*: 'Morecambe and Wise are to leave the Windmill by mutual consent.' The idea was to persuade people that we hadn't been sacked but were really moving on to higher things. I doubt if it fooled anyone.

Much later when the Windmill was celebrating some sort of anniversary we were asked if our names could be included on an honorary roll-call of performers who had started out at the theatre. A plaque would be fixed to the building listing artists who had the Windmill to thank for their successes. When we were approached I took great pleasure in reminding the legendary VD that he had fired us. His reaction to my suggestion as to what he might do with his roll-call of honour must sadly go unrecorded.

Meanwhile our last few days of 'exposure' were rapidly coming to an end and our plan to attract agents wasn't amounting to much. The one and only agent to turn up was a man called Gordon Norval who had two show dates on his books, the Grand, Clapham and the Empire, Kilburn. They weren't the best dates but they were significantly better than nothing at all. Norval watched us perform and agreed to take us on.

'Can you do the Clapham Grand on Monday?' he asked.

I took out my diary, scrutinised its blindingly blank pages and hummed quizzically. 'I think we might just be free that night, Mr Norval,' I said, 'Yes, I think we can offer you that one.'

'Good. I'll give you £25 a week. Can you do two spots?'

'Yes, of course,' we lied. We had only twelve minutes of material between us and even slowing it down wouldn't stretch it much further.

'Good,' said Norval, 'I'll make it £27 10s.'

And that was that. We were half elated, half appalled. While we now had a toe-hold in the big time we knew with grisly clarity that our routine was only enough for one spot. We were being paid for two. A yawning, ten-minute chasm of silence was opening before us. In just under a week's time we were due to step into the mainstream of professional variety and, after ten years in the business, we did not have an act.

^{ORCHID}^{ROOM} CENTRAL PIER BLACKPOOL

| SUMMER SHOW OPENING DATE | SATURDAY JUNE 1st 1957 | 6·10 & 8·30 TWICE NIGHTLY MATINEE THURS 2·30 |

'LETS HAVE FUN'

MORECAMBE AND WISE
TV AND RADIO COMEDIANS

JOAN TURNER
THE GIRL WITH A THOUSAND VOICES

MAUREEN ROSE
B.B.C. SINGER

THREE DEUCES
CANADA'S AMBASSADORS OF RHYTHM

THE THREE BELLES

EDDIE GRANT
THE NEW STAR COMIC

THE ORCHID ROOM LOVELIES

KENNY BAKER
BRITAIN'S "ACE" TRUMPETER

DENNIS SPICER
TV AND RADIO STAR

BOOK NOW! 5/- 4/- RESERVED

BOX OFFICE MANAGER. CENTRAL PIER BLACKPOOL.

5

Splendours and Miseries

Panic, now that Sadie had gone, was the mother of our invention. As soon as we had the contract in our pocket we raced back home to Mrs Duer's, locked ourselves away in our room, and began to work on a second routine. We thought back to all the Abbott and Costello we had seen, mentally rerunning each film for a gag to plunder. We cast our minds back to all the acts we had heard and watched from the wings, trying to remember the jokes that had got the laughs. We consulted what books and notes we had, desperately searching out potential material we could hammer into our own shape.

When we were in our early teens, as young discoveries eager for new ideas, we regularly stole other people's stuff. The sole criterion was whether it went down well. Whether we understood it was neither here nor there. So it was that we incorporated into our forthcoming second spot a joke we hadn't used for years – largely because for a long time we were too naive to understand it:

Eric comes on stage with hand on hip, mincing as he walks. I say to him, 'Where are you going?'

He answers, 'Don't be so nosy. I'm a businessman.'

'But a businessman doesn't walk like that.'

'You don't know my business.'

In it went. Along with another old faithful involving Eric coming on stage with a vase on his shoulder. I look at him and ask, 'What's that?'

'It's a Grecian urn' he replies.

'What's a Grecian earn?'

'About £2 a week.'

It was all very thin stuff and what it lacked in quality it also lacked in quantity. Here we were on the threshold of the big time, landed with a make-or-break opportunity and we couldn't deliver.

We worked night and day on that act, determined to come up with a creditable routine before the deadline. And then, although heavily disguised, inspiration struck. We hit on the idea of developing something called 'The Woody Woodpecker's Song' into a running gag.

In principle it was ridiculously simple. On stage I would tell Eric that I was going to teach him a song in which he would have the most important role. I was to keep on stressing that his part in it was crucial to the success of the act so he needed to come in at just the right moment. Then I launched into the song which was quite long and was clearly a vehicle for *me* to show off. At the end of the song there was a six-note refrain which Eric could whistle or hum in a funny voice. The idea, of course, was that Eric was fooled into thinking that he had the starring role in the song when in fact he was limited to this six-note pay-off.

It was a classically simple idea but one which at the time we did not set too much store by. After all, this was to be our second spot – we were really being paid for our first. We worked on the Woodpecker routine at home, filled it out with a bit of back-chat, added a couple of gags either side and finally had a second spot which we felt we could get away with.

We made our way apprehensively to the Grand, Clapham on an unpromising Monday night and got into our first routine, which went down quite badly. We were not encouraged. Fully expecting our second spot to do worse than the first we came on after the interval only to find that the audience loved it. Loved it. We had the whole theatre in the palm of our hands with that one song.

The great thing about it, once it had got its first laugh, was that the tension grew during subsequent verses, with the result that the laughter was always louder than the last time and, since the audience knew what to expect, it could share in the build-up to the comedy. As I sang the main part the audience became increasingly amused watching Eric pulling impatient faces in the background. The six-note pay-off was a delicious release and produced great waves of applause which brought the house down.

The reaction didn't go unnoticed by the management, nor by the agents and bookers who were also in that Monday night audience. In our business all you have to do is go up there and do well and everybody wants you. The real trick is staying there.

We were booked straight away – 'act as seen' – for the following week at the Empire, Kilburn where we decided to reverse the order of the two spots. The Woody Woodpecker's Song got the audience on our side immediately and put us in credit for our second spot which, by now, was going down quite well.

The whole act got us continuous work for more than a month – the most we had ever worked since our circus days – and with the money we were earning we settled our outstanding bills with Mrs Duer and began to feel we were getting somewhere at last. Although the two of us were unaware of it at the time, this was the moment when the tide turned for Morecambe and Wise.

But, as with tides, our fortunes turned slowly. Our rise was not meteoric, our success did not come overnight. Instead our development was gradual, spanning twenty years during which time we were ceaselessly consolidating and extending our act.

Before we began to come to prominence on TV there was minimum glamour and maximum graft which took their toll on both of us. Ever since Eric had been discharged from the mines with heart trouble we knew that his health was not all it could have been. This business, with its peculiar mixture of physical and emotional exertion, its endless tours, and constant travelling, makes tremendous demands on a performer, even when he is in the best of health.

From 1950 to 1968 when Eric had his first heart attack we were working our hardest, sacrificing our time, our personal life and even, as it turned out, our health, for the sake of getting on in this compulsive thing we call showbusiness. Looking back at the course and intensity of our joint career, Eric's heart attack seems an almost inescapable outcome of our commitment to the profession and it was, as I think Eric said at the time, nature's way of telling us both to slow down.

*

In 1950, however, buoyant with our new-found success, we were in no mood to slow down. At this time I was still writing to Doreen Blythe, the attractive young dancer I had met in Lord John Sanger's outfit. More than that, we were going steady and she suggested to a man named Reggie Dennis that Eric and I would be useful additions to his touring revue, 'Front Page Personalities'. He liked our act and offered us almost a year's continual employment at £27 10s plus travelling expenses. It was good money and with it, more importantly, we were also earning some respect.

Until this point we had been treated as no more than jobbing comics brought in to fill a hole in the bill with the odd pantomime appearance at venues like the Opera House, Leicester or the Grand Theatre, Brighton. I remember playing Jack and the Beanstalk at the Grand for the Lupino-Lanes who were a sort of theatrical dynasty, very big in the business, and rather dismissive of the pair of us. They used to get a lot of pleasure from taking the mickey out of the two of us in front of the rest of the cast.

At one point, for example, I had to come on stage in ballet dancer's tights. Now, as you know, these things make one rather prominent out front, shall we say, and being a shy young fellow I automatically put my straw hat over the bulge.

'Come on, Wise, put your hat on! Let's see what you've got'

5. *Splendours and Miseries*

came bellowing out of the auditorium, making me extremely embarrassed and giving the assembled cast a good laugh at my expense. That particular brand of cruelty that some old-timers reserve for newcomers made our time there very uncomfortable. What a long run in 'Front Page Personalities' succeeded in doing was putting all those unhappy memories into the past and developing self-confidence in the pair of us as performers in our own right.

'Good poets borrow, great poets steal!' Didn't T.S. Eliot say that? If he did, I certainly know what he meant. If he didn't he should have done. We did the same, basing a lot of our early routines on material that had got laughs for our idols of the time, Abbott and Costello. There was a counting gag they used which we copied, adding our own elaborations to suit the audience:

Eric is counting out money to pay me back what he owes – 'One pound, two pounds, three, four, five, six ...' Then he says to me, 'How long have you been married?'

'Fifteen years.'

'Really ... fifteen, sixteen, seventeen ... you must be getting on a bit by now. How old are you?'

'Forty-eight.'

'Really ... forty-eight, forty-nine, fifty. Here it is – fifty quid. Don't bother to count it.'

Because the Woody Woodpecker routine was working so well for us in the first spot we began to relax more and were able to devote more attention to honing down our delivery of the lines rather than constantly panicking about the content. Comparatively simple cross-talk could thus acquire a lot of polish:

Eric: I came home last night and my wife was sitting up in bed crying.
Ernie: What had happened?
Eric: We'd had a burglar. So I said, 'Did he get much?'
Ernie: What did she say?
Eric: She said, 'Yes, I thought it was you.'

5. *Splendours and Miseries*

We had a lot of patter like that which can sound hard going on the page but which we could lift if we got the delivery right.

Eric: I had one of those quiet weddings.
Ernie: What do you mean?
Eric: I didn't go!
Ernie: How did you meet your wife?
Eric: At a dance. I can see her now on the ballroom floor – lying flat out, she was.
Ernie: What did you do?
Eric: I gave her mouth-to-mouth recreation.
Ernie: You mean resuscitation. Recreation is when you have fun.
Eric: That's what I mean. I'm no mug. But you should see her brother.
Ernie: What's he like?
Eric: He was staying with me last week. I told him to treat the house as if it was his.
Ernie: And did he?
Eric: Yes, he sold it this morning.

Now, we had been using some of this kind of material for a quite a while and when we were raw beginners it didn't go down terribly well. What was gradually happening was a subtle change in our emphasis here or in our facial expression there, and it made all the difference. As we got better and better we stopped pinching other people's material and started having the confidence to invent for ourselves.

*

We also had the confidence to vary the pace. Eric had a standing joke that if the management wanted a nine-minute spot all we had to do was speak a bit more quickly and if they wanted fifteen minutes' worth we just had to slow down the delivery. The secret was in the timing.

And yet despite our growing confidence and the security of a long run we were by no means guaranteed uniform success wherever we appeared. We still had to take the rough with the smooth and at the wide variety of dates we played, there was enough 'rough' to prevent us from losing our heads.

If we got a Monday night audience, possibly a quarter full, and had to go on second after a troupe of girl dancers we had one hell of a job warming them up. There were many times when we did a whole comedy routine in complete silence. The moment that happened was the moment when our hard-won confidence could fail us.

Failure generated fear and fear generated paralysis. We stood there motionless with glazed looks trying to gabble out our words while our mouths got drier and drier. When we sensed that things were going badly we speeded up the routine just to get the whole painful experience over as quickly as possible.

Speeding things up without telling the orchestra, however, had its problems. We always went off with a big rousing number, as all comics did in order to leave the audience with a powerful last impression of the act. If we compressed our twelve-minute act into six – which we sometimes did – we had, of course, to bring our finale forward by six minutes.

The trouble was that the orchestra, anxious not to lose a moment's drinking time, would write on their song copies after the first song: 'Twelve minutes to finale', which meant twelve minutes in which to nip to the bar for a pint. The musicians had it timed to the second.

So Eric and I, by now at the end of our routine and ready to go into the big finish, would look down into the pit and see, with horror, that there was nobody there. The Musical Director, who would be keeping an ear on the performance, would then realise himself what was happening, bring in whoever he could and play us out with whatever instruments he could call on.

Many a time we would do our big finish to the thin notes of a piano and one violin. It was terrifying. Back in the dressing room we would try to rationalise it all, of course:

'Wasn't too bad really given the audience we had.'

'That lot out there probably had a hard day.'

'We'd have been all right if only the microphone ... the band ... the Musical Director ... etc etc.'

There was a definite pattern to the variety audiences in those days, making some nights a more frightening prospect than others. For instance, Monday night first house was always as tough as nails. With the working week only just begun and with a full four or five days of it still to look forward to the audience was in a difficult mood.

Performances which followed half-day closing were hard going, too. The audience would be composed of business people, quite well-off folk who had a measure of sophistication and who had seen it all before. They sat there challenging us, daring us to entertain them. On Friday and Saturday night, by contrast, we could do no wrong. With the prospect of a weekend off, people were relaxed and happy and were on our side from the moment we stepped out on stage.

*

Even though we were doing two spots twice nightly it amounted only to something like three-quarters of an hour's work – not a great deal when it was spread out over an evening which began around 6 pm and ended at 10.30. It could be quite a lonely life in its way: arriving half an hour before curtain up, dressing, doing the make-up and hearing the plaintive sound of the band tuning up. That could be a pretty sad sound when we were stuck in some provincial second-rate joint doing medium-to-bad business on a cold and wet Monday evening.

The bill usually opened with a fast dance routine with an act like 'Linda and Lana' – two girls who always worked up to a really quick finish to get the audience primed for our appearance. The applause would slow down. There would be a 'tap-tap' from the MD, and he would then go into the opening bars of our act. Twelve minutes later we were off, hanging around until our second spot.

5. *Splendours and Miseries*

The pattern was repeated for the second house, then we went home. The big danger for some of the pros could be taking off for a long session in the pub to while away the hours between performances. We were never drinkers, so fortunately that was never one of the temptations.

The order of appearance was decided by the management, and a little electric sign, rather like a hymn board in church, would signal the next act from the side of the stage. As it flashed up 'Act II', 'Act III' and so on, the audience consulted their sixpenny programmes to connect the act with the name.

We all had descriptive bill matter on the programme to give a thumb-nail sketch of our act and alert the audience, in a cryptic way, as to what to expect. 'Morecambe and Wise: fools rush in', for example. A light violinist might be billed a 'fiddling and fooling'. It was the printed equivalent of the signature tune, a little piece of headline matter to reinforce our professional identity.

In the Fifties there would often be an eight-act bill. Dancers first, then a comic, possibly a juggler next, followed by a singer, a speciality act, a magician, a ventriloquist and a big name to finish. The second half would see a similar permutation leading up to the moment when the big name, top-of-the-bill, would make his entry.

This was usually the only time when the master of ceremonies made a formal announcement: 'Ladies and Gentlemen, the moment you have all been waiting for ...' – very encouraging for the rest of us, that – 'direct from the London Palladium, Lena Horne', or Joseph Locke, or whoever.

*

There were odd independent variety theatres in various parts of the country, but most would belong to a circuit of theatres of which the largest and most prestigious were without a doubt the Moss Empires. There was the Nottingham Empire, for example, the Leeds Empire, the Liverpool Empire and so on, which were all recognised as very big dates to play. But of these the Finsbury Park Empire in London was reckoned to be the best of the lot – a real showcase for the big league acts.

The presiding genius over these sought-after venues was a formidable woman by the name of Cissy Williams – the head booker for all the Moss Empires. It was advisable to keep well in with her and on no account cross her because she wielded terrifying power.

In addition to the gloom of the Monday night house, artists had to face the weekly check-up by the manager. He would sit out front, watch the acts and note down comments. These he put into a report which found itself on Cissy Williams's desk later in the week.

If an act died on its feet he would inform Cissy that it wasn't worth the £35 a week it was getting. The act then had until Wednesday to do something about it. If it had picked up by the time the manager did his second inspection, all was well. If it hadn't, then the artists were informed that they were coming off at the end of the week. In rare cases they could be pulled at a moment's notice.

In one celebrated incident, retold by Harry Secombe, his own act was taken off as a result of a misunderstanding. Harry had a routine which required him to come on stage shaving – he had used it at the Windmill in his early days. On the Monday evening a new manager had taken a cursory glance at the gag and decided to fire him on the spot. Harry protested, but to no effect. The reason given was simple: 'I'm not having him shaving in my bloody time. He's fired!'

It was inadvisable to have too many failures, of course, and all the pros in the business would be extremely careful to talk only of their successes. Failures, too, had to be seen in the best possible light and described selectively. Like the two pros who got talking about their recent work:

'Oh yes', says the first, 'I was in Manchester a couple of weeks ago. Went down really well. Standing ovation every night. Then I was off to Leeds and the same again. Sensational. Three curtain calls. Couldn't go wrong. Then I followed that with Bradford.'

'Oh, wait a minute,' says the second, 'I was on that bill with you.'

'Really?' says the first, losing confidence now, 'God, they were a tough audience, weren't they?'

Some of these stories are certainly of doubtful origin, but they do illustrate abiding truths in the business. One of them concerns a double act that splits and meets up again in Charing Cross Road at their former agent's office.

'What are you doing at the moment?' asks one.

'Oh, marvellous stuff. I'm touring second top in a smash hit. It's breaking all records.'

'Really?' says the other, 'I didn't hear about that.'

'Yes, I've just made a single and it's working its way nicely up the hit parade.'

'Really? Now, I didn't know that.'

'And I'm off next week to play the Talk of the Town.'

'I didn't hear about that either.'

'But I'll tell you something. I was at the Palladium a fortnight ago and died the death.'

'Oh, yes, I heard about that.'

Bad news has a habit of travelling extremely fast, and it is wise for artists to avoid all contact with it.

*

If a particular variety bill had a distinct shape to it, variety in general imposed an equally distinct pattern on our life. Typically we arrived in town on Sunday night having travelled all day by train or, later, when we were earning more, by car, and we found our digs. These had usually been passed on to us by fellow pros. If they were entirely new we made a careful note for future reference.

We trembled on arrival if we opened the visitors' book to see in the comments column the words 'I shall certainly tell my friends.' This was the universally accepted code for 'This is a really terrible joint.' On other occasions the comment 'It makes you appreciate home' was a more direct way of saying the same thing.

5. *Splendours and Miseries*

By ten o'clock next morning we were at the theatre for the ritual band call or rehearsal. We went along with our band books containing all the numbers we had in the act complete with notes, timings, variations and orchestrations and placed them on the stage.

There was a strict sequence to this. Those first with the band books rehearsed first, those second in line rehearsed second and so on. I have even known some people to come in the night before and set their band books down on the stage a good twelve hours before anybody else: just to rehearse first and be away.

The only permitted variation on this pattern would be if the top-of-the-bill chose discreetly to pull rank. 'Does anybody mind if I go first? I have a broadcast at midday' was a typical queue-jumping ploy. Of course, everybody in the auditorium minded but we all nodded understandingly. After all, it might just be our turn to jump the queue some day.

There was a terrible pecking order in variety. If you were given a small billing, you had to learn to know your place. If you were top, you could afford to call the tune, and there were very few top-of-the-bills who were above pulling rank when they needed to.

Band call was at 11 am. That lasted a couple of hours or so, depending on the length and type of act on the bill. Comics, by and large, were soon over. We had the least to do and once the opening number and the big finish were rehearsed we were free. Singers might take a little longer to get exactly the right sound out of the band or to haggle with the MD about how best to arrange a particular song.

*

The other advantage of being comics was that we could always travel light. Some of the speciality acts had to carry trunkloads of gear wherever they went. Henry Vadden, for example, had a sensational finish to an act of his. He put on a Prussian spiked helmet and then produced a huge cartwheel

92

from the wings. He spun it round and round, flung it up high into the air and caught it on the spike of his helmet.

Years of performing this act had left him with a very short neck. It was a fabulous finale, but can you imagine having to pack a cartwheel in your luggage every time you caught a train from Grimsby to the Glasgow Empire?

Other people were the same. Tattersall and Jerry, for example, was a wonderful ventriloquism act. Tattersall was a good vent, but an even better craftsman, and was singlehandedly responsible for building his own lifesize dummies. Now you can picture for yourself how much space a couple of those would take up in an Austin 7. At least we were spared that.

As a consequence Tattersall was involved in the kind of mishap we could never have encountered. Whereas we used the bare minimum of props he went in for them in a big way, which was hazardous because, as we all came to realise, props could have an independent life of their own.

The dummies Tattersall made were huge and very convincing. They were driven mechanically and could walk and, apparently, breathe. He, of course, did the talking for them.

One of his routines involved him in a song, 'My Old Dutch'. Two dummies, one an old man, the other an old woman, made an appearance upstage on either side of him. Then slowly, under their own steam, they moved downstage towards him as he sang the song, 'We've been together now for forty years and it don't seem a day too much ... ' Sadly for him the slope of the stage at the Theatre Royal was too steep for the act, and a minute into it it became clear to the audience, if not to Tattersall, that the dummies were accelerating their pace to a degree incompatible with their supposed geriatric status.

By the time Tattersall himself realised, they were already rolling past him towards the edge of the stage and even a last-minute lunge by him could not prevent them from toppling into the orchestra pit and almost braining half the brass section.

93

5. Splendours and Miseries

The speciality acts in those days were marvellously inventive and highly unusual. Perhaps the most famous was a sand-dance performed in an Egyptian setting by Wilson, Keppel and Betty. They came on in cut-down Pharaoh's robes, sprinkled sand on a board and slipped and slid around on it in time to a special arrangement from the band.

Then there were the Wonder Wheelers, a top-class bicycle act; the Berganjo Brothers and Juanita, an acrobatic act; Nino and his Wonder Dog, which involved a dog coming on stage propelling a huge ball beneath its feet and leaping off a high parapet into Nino's arms.

There was Roger Carne, a ventriloquist who used to come on as a drunk and engage in conversation with a cat on his shoulder. There was a tiny woman with a trapeze act called La Petite Poupée. There were the Two Pirates who had an act which apparently involved them in gravity-defying acrobatics. They spun and leapt around the stage until in one colossal bound one of them dived at the other coming to rest vertically and balancing forefinger to forefinger, one on top of the other. Close scrutiny revealed a cunning series of almost invisible supporting wires. The audience were in on the joke, shouting 'Oh yes there is!' to the Pirates' 'Oh no there isn't!'

There were Indian club acts, wirewalkers, fire-eaters, puppeteers, chimpanzees and one famous bear act we worked with called Vogelwein's Bears. Vogelwein was a huge mountain of a man, a German, who got his bears to ride bicycles and balance balls. Now, there was no question of his boarding the train to Cardiff at the last minute with an act like that. Travel had to be scrupulously arranged in advance, the animals had to be fed and they had to be safely locked away. A couple of comics like ourselves had an easy life by comparison.

The advantage the speciality acts had over us was that they had no need to alter their routine at all. Whereas we had to adapt and add and refine our material constantly, someone like Henry Vadden only ever needed a German helmet and a cartwheel. That was all the public was coming to see him do.

An act like Wilson, Keppel and Betty, for example, survived

absolutely unchanged for twenty years. Wilson and Keppel stayed together (although there were lots of Bettys over the years) and merely continued the sole routine for which they were known. It was so popular that they were able to make their living by it for all that time. The ten-minute sand dance was a never-ending source of pleasure – and income.

*

After the band call we had the day to ourselves before the first house of the week at six o'clock that evening. Our dressing rooms, if never palatial, were adequate and served as a rudimentary home-from-home for the rest of the run. Just as the landladies' visiting book contained coded messages for the initiated, so too did the dressing room. The management had polite notices pinned up by every washbasin, such as: 'LADIES PLEASE DO NOT WASH OFF YOUR WET-WHITE IN THE SINK. THIS CAN LEAD TO ACCIDENTS.'

Those familiar with theatrical lore knew immediately that this message was designed to appeal to men as much as to women. Wet-white was a kind of body make-up the girls used to apply to their legs and arms before going on stage, and the main force of the notice was as a reminder to them not to clog the basin with it.

But pros could easily spot the subtext of the message which said, though clearly not in so many words, 'GENTLEMEN, PLEASE DO NOT PEE IN THE SINK.' If an act had a dressing room on the ground floor and the gents was on the third, however, the injunction was rarely heeded.

Monday night gave way to Tuesday morning and, in turn, to the second of the week's fixed points – the post mortem at the Kardomah Coffee Shop. All the acts would gather in the Kardomah to read the write-ups in the local paper.

The foremost theatrical critic of the day was a man named Hannan Swaffer, and it naturally followed that every cub reporter on every small-town newspaper wanted to make his name as the future Hannan Swaffer. They came along on

Monday night on complimentary tickets provided by the manager and proceeded to pen their impressions.

Of Harry Worth it was said, 'He will be a very funny performer once he gets over his nerves' – an observation which completely missed the point. Nervousness, worked at, rehearsed and perfected, was the essence of his act. And of us it was once said, 'Morecambe and Wise have the ball of showbusiness at their feet.'

These lads had to be very careful about giving offence. The critics weren't allowed to get away with the sort of abuse that passes for criticism nowadays. Many times we saw the top-of-the-bill so incensed by a comparatively harmless remark by some junior reporter that the young lad was summoned to the theatre the next day to apologise. The top-of-the-bill used to have a lot of clout in those days. For the rest of us, though, it was rather different.

A pall of gloom hung over the Kardomah if the write-ups were bad. Of course, if they were good, elation spread throughout the cast and we were able to look forward to the coming week with confidence. But either way the shared experience of the ups and downs, the splendour and the misery, forged a Kardomah camaraderie which lasted for years to come.

Once the first two days were over the week's routine became quite pleasant. In those days the cinemas and theatres had reciprocal arrangements for complimentary tickets. In exchange for free seats at the variety, performers were given a card which entitled them to go to the pictures for nothing. Wilkie Bard was an old artist of the time and since his name rhymed with card he became variety rhyming-slang for a free afternoon at the cinema – 'I went to see Chaplin on the Wilkie' became the form of words we adopted. For years I used to sit in empty cinemas in the afternoons whiling away the hours before performances.

*

1. At home, June 1990.

2. At school in the 1930s. I am bottom left, about to break into my Al Jolson impression.

3. Influenced by Charlie Chaplin? Aged 12.

4. My dad, Harry Wiseman. Now you know where I get my sartorial elegance.

5. Born to be a star (note the clogs). Aged about 12.

6. What a personality! Aged 12.

7. A sophisticated double act. Eric and I with traditional straw hats.

8. In the Merchant Navy, 1945, keeping the sea lanes open between the Tyne and the Thames.

9. With Doreen, Eric and Joan and their children at Weymouth in the 1950s.

10. Setting off to receive the OBE at Buckingham Palace with my mother and Doreen.

Reference: 35/TS   14th March, 1960

Dear Morecambe and Wise,

    Thank you for letting me see the
enclosed synopsis. The 'double' idea is, of
course, always good value but I would not be
too certain that it would work effectively on
Television without involving quite an amount
of prefilming. Unfortunately we just do not
have a space available at this moment for this
idea but if an opportunity should arise we
will get in touch with you.

              Yours sincerely,

              (Tom Sloan)
    Assistant Head of Light Entertainment,
             Television.

Messrs. Morecambe & Wise,
24 Thorpe Avenue,
Peterborough,
Northants.

11. One of our many rejections.

12. With the Beatles in 1962. They were guests on one of our ATV shows.

13. With George Brown, 'I'm in show business too', at the Labour Party Conference at Blackpool in 1961.

14. Spot the stars (Des O'Connor, Jimmy Edwards, Cliff Richard and many more). Blackpool artistes, 1961.

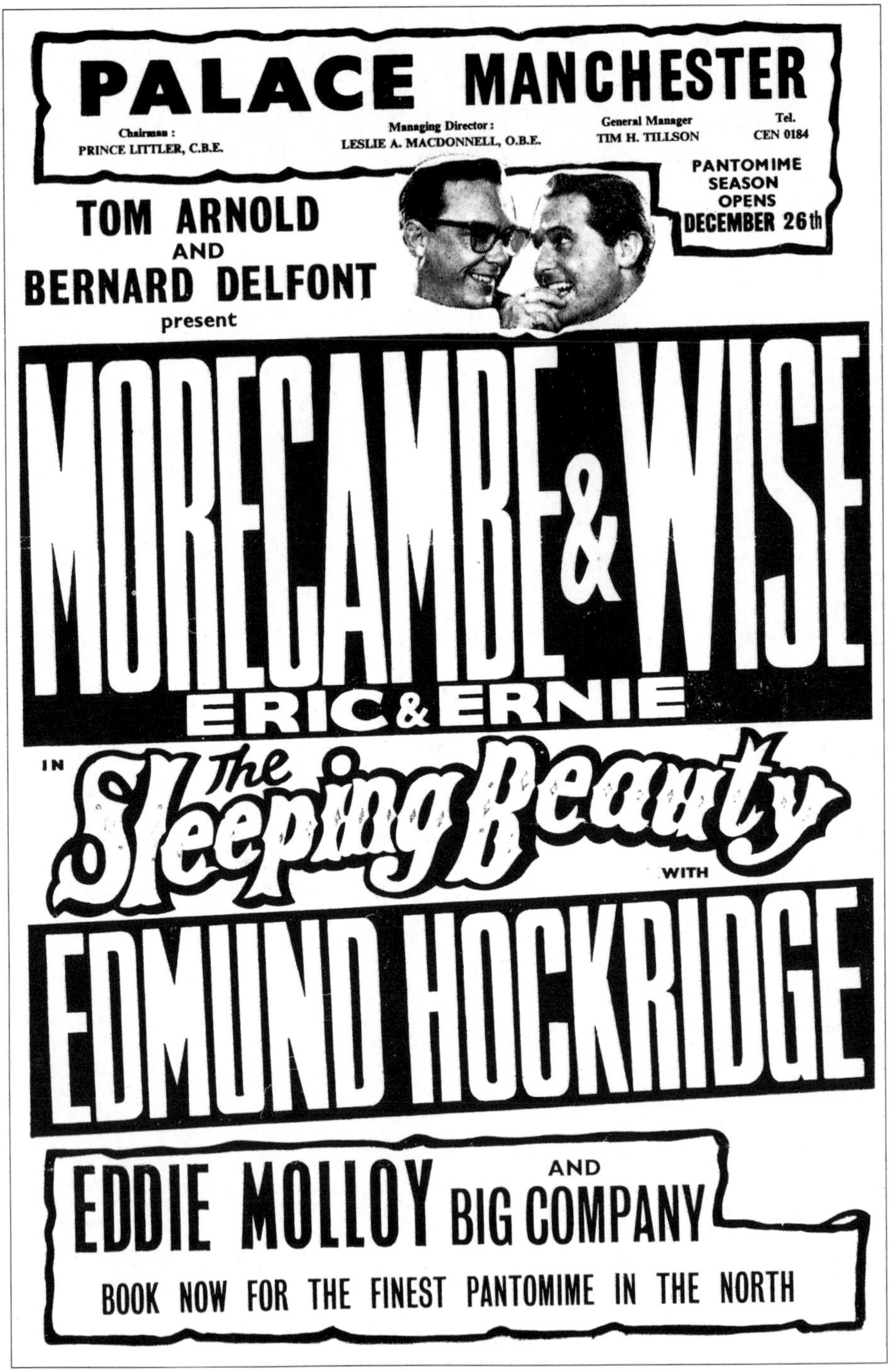

15. Pantomime bill, 1964.

16. In Bermuda en route to New York for Ed Sullivan's show.

17. 'The Fleet's In' with Cliff Richard.

18. Looking for trouble. With Sean Connery on the set of *That Riviera Touch* at Pinewood in 1968.

19. With Michael Aspel: 'Don't do it Michael! I loved your last show.'

20. With Vanessa Redgrave: 'Take your hand off my wallet!'

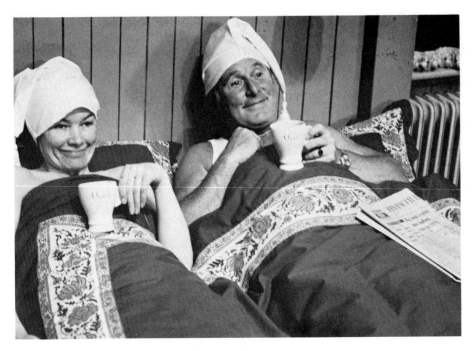

21. In bed with Glenda Jackson. Don't tell the *News of the World!*

22. With Glenda as Cleopatra, doing the famous sand dance.

23. With Robin Day: 'You wouldn't hit a man with glasses . . .'.

24. 'Hey Big Spender.' I've got the best legs but the bar was 3 inches too high.

25. Cartoon strip from *Reveille*, 11th June 1976.

26. With Diana Rigg as Nell Gwynne on the bed that kept going up and down (see p. 154).

27. With my agent, Billy Marsh.

28. Garden party at Thames TV, including (seated, left to right) Judith Chalmers, Max Bygraves, Paul Eddington, Nanette Newman, Denis Norden, Bryan Cowgill (head of Thames) and Lionel Blair with the champagne.

29. A chorus line with Sir Ralph Richardson, baffled to the end (see pp. 146-7).

30. 'We always fly British Airways.'

31. What it takes to put on a show, and that's not including the orchestra! Cast and crew of one of our shows for Thames TV.

32. With our old friend Tommy Cooper.

33. With Ian Ogilvy and Susannah York in a play wot I wrote.

34. With our friend Marion Montgomery.

35. With Jimmy Tarbuck, Des O'Connor, Bruce Forsyth and Mike Yarwood at the 'Bring Me Sunshine' tribute to Eric at the London Palladium, 1984.

36. With HRH Prince Philip at the 'Bring Me Sunshine' tribute to Eric.

37. My big solo attempt. With Lulu and Julia Hills on the last night of 'The Mystery of Edwin Drood' at the Savoy Theatre, 4 July 1987. It should never have closed.

38. 'Be careful where you put your hands, girls!' With Lulu and Julia Hills.

39. In 1989 I flew round the world in 80 hours to raise money for a heart charity called Corda, dressed as Phileas Fogg with Marty Christian of the New Seekers as my manservant.

40. In Sydney during my successful solo tour of Australia in 1985.

41. Receiving an award from the Queen Mother.

42. With Peter Barkworth, Lady Falkender and Doreen at a Variety Club lunch.

43. Doreen and I sample the seafood in Perth, Australia, 1985.

44. At home in Hollywood on Thames.

5. Splendours and Miseries

There was never any need for rehearsal during the week because the act didn't change. The acrobats would practise most days to keep themselves in trim and we would usually hear musicians doing the same. But comics were a different proposition and were regarded as a pretty lazy bunch.

The Fifties were a straight-laced decade for comedians. We had to be very careful with our material and aware of the acceptable limits within which we could work. The only swear-word we could use was 'bloody', and it was advisable not to be too liberal with it otherwise the manager would come round with instructions for us to tone things down a bit. It was still very funny at that time to talk about belly buttons, and peeing and knickers (pretty basic stuff, I admit, and very passé today), but if we used any of these ideas in the routine we couldn't refer to any of them by name.

The actual words were taboo, though we could be suggestive by using words which rhymed. We only had to say 'I knew a young lady called Nelly' to get guffaws from all over the audience. 'I wish I were a caterpillar, life would be a farce, I'd climb up all the plants and trees, and slide down on my ... hands and knees' would produce gales of laughter from an audience sharing in disappointed, but knowing, anticipation. They were very innocent times.

For years we did a routine which relied on the deliberate double-entendre of 'wiggling', i.e. peeing. I was to teach Eric to be a pop singer. I began a song, and got him to join in. Then I said: 'Now at this point you start wiggling.'

'What?' asks Eric looking with feigned shock at the audience.

We always got a laugh here.

'You wiggle. You start to wiggle.'

More laughter follows as Eric merely looks at the audience saying nothing. Then he turns to me as if whispering and says:

'In front of all this lot?'

And so the gag went on, drawing great big belly laughs from the audience every time we so much as mentioned the word. Nothing was explicit, all was suggested.

After a time we also began to 'feel' an audience, to know what

97

type of material would go down well and to extend it accordingly. The 'wiggling' gag, for example, we could milk for all we felt it was worth.

If our weekly routine as performers was pleasant enough there were three words which could spoil our mood at a stroke. They struck fear into the most hardened of performers: The Glasgow Empire.

When we got that booking we blanched, knowing it to be the graveyard of English comics. Indeed, so famous was it for its frosty welcomes that Cissy Williams gave everyone an extra ten pounds for doing the date. The Glaswegians loved American singers as top-of-the-bill but loathed most other things, reserving a special distaste for comedians from south of the border.

The experience of Des O'Connor is probably the classic. He went on to do his routine and found himself facing what was an increasingly hostile audience. As we had done in the past, he started to speed up the act, and gabble his words. Then he lost track of the tag, forgot where he was and his mouth dried. All the time he was alone on the stage with nobody able to help.

At least a double act like ours ensures that each performer has some moral support from the other, but Des had no one. In the end he did the only logical thing. He fainted. A couple of disembodied hands appeared from under the curtains and he was pulled off stage, legs first, under the tabs. Another victim of the Glasgow Empire.

For a long time Eric used to do a gag among pros at parties. It went: 'I will now do an impression of Des O'Connor doing second spot at the Glasgow Empire, "Ladies and Gentlemen ... THUD!"'

Two other very experienced comedians got the same treatment. One was Jimmy Edwards. Half way through his act a guy from the third row shouted out, 'Why don't you just f... off?'

To which Jimmy replied in genuine shock, 'I beg your pardon.'

Then a voice from the back of the auditorium shouted, 'You heard what my friend said. Why don't you just f... off?'

5. Splendours and Miseries

It was just such audience solidarity which nearly undid Jimmy James when he was performing there in the Fifties. He had a ten-minute act which was going down so badly that he decided to cut it short. He was on just before the top-of-the-bill, an American singer.

After five minutes he brought his patter to a close and walked off stage to the sound of his own footsteps. In the wings the American top was putting the last-minute touches to his costume fully expecting to be given a couple of minutes to get himself ready. Unprepared he said to Jimmy, 'Hey, what's going on?'

To which Jimmy replied, 'You are,' and dashed off to his dressing room.

*

An empty stage is a very lonely place. When the act is going well, though, there is nowhere like it. And when it's going very well it's advisable not to interfere. We learnt a useful lesson in leaving things as they are when we were working with Val Parnell at the Prince of Wales much later in our careers.

We had done our first spot and it had gone down well. During the interval they told us that the show was overrunning and asked us to cut a couple of minutes off the act. Like good little boys we did. But we were then left with a very unbalanced routine which was far from successful and, as a result, we weren't invited back for quite a while.

When we next performed there the same thing happened and because of the overrun we were asked once again to cut back on our material. By now we had learnt from our mistake. We went on for our second spot and started to get the laughs. So much so that we carried on, ignoring the overrun and came off to huge applause, only to find Val Parnell in the wings afterwards giving us a dressing down. 'What do you think you're doing, boys, overrunning like that? It's disgraceful,' or words to that effect.

We took the tirade politely enough, but we also took it with a

99

pinch of salt. The golden rule is simple. If you're doing well, stay there. There's nothing the buggers can do short of bringing the curtain down on you, and if you're entertaining the public they're hardly likely to do that, are they? If you're doing well, make the most of it. They won't want to know you the moment you're doing badly.

Obviously we had to keep this within reason and we never set out deliberately to overrun. For one thing it was unfair on everybody else and, for another, if the show went beyond a certain point the band was on overtime which costs a lot of money.

Nor was it advisable to take the overrun to the insane proportions that Herschel Henlere had taken it. His act was a show stopper, a speciality act which involved his dressing up as a Mad Professor and playing the piano and assorted instruments at a furious pace. The crowd loved it.

We were sharing the bill with him very early on in our careers and from the wings we were watching him go through his routine to great effect. As the act went on – and on – it was clear he wasn't going to leave the stage at all. Eventually, in despair, the manager brought the curtain down on him.

But even that did not deter him. Instead he grabbed an accordion, scampered underneath the curtain and did an impromptu act in front of the tabs. He wasn't a popular man for the rest of the run and, though I think he overdid it on this occasion, it was easy to understand what was going through his mind. If the audience likes you, let them have it, because they'll very soon tell you when they've had enough.

A variant on this piece of theatrical wisdom was offered to us in 1948 at the Town Hall, Watford by none other than the greatest Music Hall comic of the day, Max Miller. We were at the outset of our career then and, for some reason, Max took a shine to us. He was very kind and helpful, and as he was about to go on stage one night he turned to me and said, 'Don't forget, lad, in this business when one door shuts, they all bloody shut.' Hardly surprising, then, that Herschel Henlere was determined to make the most of his moment of glory.

5. *Splendours and Miseries*

Very occasionally, though, we were actually *asked* to lengthen our spot. I remember once playing on a variety bill with the zither player Anton Karas. Leslie Grade, the agent who had booked the bill, asked us if we could do an extra three minutes. It was apparently to make up for Anton Karas whose act only ran to seven minutes (including walking on and off) and whose repertoire that tour seemed to extend only as far as the theme tune from 'The Third Man'.

We did an act of twelve minutes and found it quite a challenge to come up with an extra three minutes to introduce Anton. We spent all day on it and concluded, as I remember, with Eric walking on stage with his coat collar turned up and looking like Harry Lime.

'I've just come out of a sewer,' he said. (Big laugh.)

'And there's this fellah playing a boring tune on a broken piano.' (Big laugh.)

*

So much for the perils and pitfalls of introducing material to pad out a sketch.

Once we were established on the variety circuit life settled down into a pleasant enough routine. We were no longer paranoid about the act, we knew what material worked well and we could sit back and consolidate our gains. We were both unmarried, so we led a carefree, bachelor life, travelling from date to date, occasionally staying with Sadie in Morecambe or with my family in Leeds.

Most of our work at this time was in the North where we both preferred to operate. It had a homely feel to it which suited our temperaments. London had what we considered unnecessary disadvantages, like performing at the Brixton Empire south of the Thames and having to commute by tube from digs in the west of the city.

A performer's diary notionally contained two fixed periods: the summer season, and autumn end-of-the-year pantomime. The big thing was to get a date at, say, the Central Pier,

101

Blackpool, between May and September and another doing pantomime at Christmas. Both seasons involved a twelve-week run apiece and, with that block of work assured, we knew we were unlikely to starve.

We had two acts: a variety act, of course, and a pantomime act which producers would buy in for the duration of the show. We might develop a captain and his mate routine which could be slipped into 'Sinbad the Sailor', or we might work on a robber routine for 'Ali Baba and the Forty Thieves', the idea being to have a distinct act which the director could incorporate into his show relatively easily. I remember one cross moment between Eric and a director, who will remain nameless, on the set of 'Babes in the Wood' in Sheffield.

We had as good as perfected a terrific fight scene which took the audience by storm. We shot at each other with guns, we duelled with swords, we dashed around the whole set wrestling and writhing, with Eric calling out to the audience to cheer when he was on top and to boo when he was underneath.

It was a very funny routine, tailor-made for pantomime, which culminated in my stabbing him, in an obviously phoney way, between his arm and his chest and him staggering around shouting, 'I'm dying.'

At this point I rushed off stage and came on again with a bucket. As he lay on the stage I held the bucket close to his leg and he kicked it. End of scene.

Well, the director in question quibbled over some of the stage business at rehearsal and suggested alterations which Eric and I thought simply didn't work. With a composed and controlled temper Eric told him that what the director had just witnessed was twenty-five years of comic know-how and experience compressed into a ten-minute routine, and that we weren't about to change it for anyone.

He was right to insist. We knew instinctively when a routine worked and, if it did, it was professional suicide to change it. 'If it ain't broke,' as the Americans say, 'don't fix it.'

*

5. Splendours and Miseries

With our summer season and pantomime booked we were now free to pencil in variety dates, club work and the occasional BBC broadcast. The Corporation was good to us, allowing us to work on scripts in our own time and to present them in a series of radio broadcasts. Radio work was a useful safety net to cushion us when we fell on relatively lean times.

It was also an opportunity to diversify. If we managed to get 'Workers' Playtime' once a month – a cut-down variety show broadcast from a factory or a mill or an office – then we were managing to keep our work rate nicely topped up.

We took anything in the early days – the important thing was simply to keep working. Even one desperate date, in a place I have long since forgotten, for a revue called 'This Is The Show'. Needless to say the initial letters of the title were displayed in bold type to give the audience an idea in advance of what to expect.

There were a couple of showgirls, a tatty five-piece band and a couple of comics – ourselves among them – involved in a bit of short-term entertainment which was none the less given the full theatrical treatment. The MC announced it all as 'glamour, excitement and fun just back from a smash hit in London brought to you live tonight ... ladies and gentlemen ...' The usual build-up.

The pair of us stuck together through the good, the bad and the ugly, but in character we were quite different. For one thing, Eric never really had much ambition. I was always the one with the push and he was happy to have it that way. I negotiated our fees, planned our seasons, worked out our dates. He was content to go along with the arrangements.

At the outset, though, ambition, for both of us, was very modest. True, we did have at the back of our minds a rather ill-defined notion of 'getting to the top', of climbing to the very last rung of the showbiz ladder, but the conscious part of our effort went into simply earning a reasonable living. The ambition was limited to having a small house, perhaps a car and getting to second top.

In practice we didn't particularly relish being top-of-the-bill

– we didn't want the responsibility. We looked round at the acts of the day and saw that they were making a perfectly acceptable living doing what they had done for years, and that seemed to suit us. Wilson, Keppel and Betty, for instance, with a sand dance that had survived unchanged for twenty years were still a crowd-puller capable of getting a regular income of something like £100 a week. In the early days that seemed a good enough future to us both.

As we progressed in the business, though, I began to be aware of more possibilities opening up around us. With the rise of television it was clearly not going to be enough to stand still. We had to develop, to move on, to extend ourselves.

That was where Eric and I differed. Of the two of us I think he was more interested in having a good time and enjoying himself, whereas I was constantly working towards a goal. Not that Eric was forever living it up – far from it, he worked unstintingly on the act – but his ambition had its boundaries. He had always been influenced by Sadie, of course, a very powerful and ambitious mother who pushed and pushed well into his teenage years.

When the two of us teamed up I became, to a certain extent, a replacement for his mother's motivation. Eric was an instinctive comedian, a born performer, a natural on the stage, but organising and planning a career went against the grain for him and he was happier to leave that side of things to someone else, to his mother in the early days, and later to me.

A lot of people used to say at the time that a double act was a risky undertaking. 'What do you do if one of you dies or if you fall out?' they used to ask us.

My answer was simple. As for the dying there was very little either of us could do about that, and falling out was unlikely because, although we were different in temperament and in our attitudes to money and career, we complemented each other. We brought different qualities to our partnership and the evidence is that the two qualities went well together. For that I am thankful.

*

5. Splendours and Miseries

The theatrical world we inhabited in the early Fifties has vanished forever. Pantomime at the Opera House, Leicester in 1950, variety at the Golders Green Hippodrome in 1951, 'Red Riding Hood' at the Dewsbury Empire, and 'Dick Whittington' at the Lyceum, Sheffield in 1952: just a few random dates from our performance diary at the time with the pair of us travelling backwards and forwards between London and provincial towns, the smallest of which would have a theatre doing reasonable business. Nowadays most of the Hippodromes, the Lyceums, the Empires, the Grands and the Tivolis have probably been transformed into cinemas or, worse still, bingo halls.

Travel between these theatres was a tiresome necessity, and we were constantly on the look-out for ways to make it more comfortable. We thought we had found the solution in the summer of 1951 when we bought a two-seater ex-Army truck from a builder in Llanelli for £125, but our hopes were to prove short-lived when frequent break-downs and the invariable mishaps when Eric took the wheel (landing in ditches, in people's front gardens, in privet hedges, that sort of thing) meant it was by no means a reliable means of locomotion.

Our second purchase was a thirty-five-seater Bedford bus which had been converted into a caravan. At first sight this seemed more promising as its advantage was that we could save money on digs. This turned out, in the end, to be just as unreliable, and in winter the accommodation section was not the most comfortable spot to seek refuge. A warm fire and a comfortable bed were infinitely preferable.

Like all pros we have had our share of theatrical digs and the formidable landladies of comic legend. Perhaps the most famous was Mrs McKay of No. 11, Daisy Avenue, Manchester. She ran very sought-after digs and was every comic's dream with her string of unintentional malapropisms.

'I've just had the place done up,' she would say. 'I've had muriels painted on the bathroom walls and pelvises fitted all along the tops of the windows.'

5. *Splendours and Miseries*

Like every landlady I have ever known, she was strict on the introduction of members of the opposite sex into guests' rooms. Her hearing was so attuned to the sound of two pairs of steps making their way upstairs in unison that she could pinpoint offenders from two rooms away with the radio playing full blast. On one occasion she became alerted to what she believed to be a suspiciously heavy tread on the stair and opened the door to see a well-known comedian walking towards his room carrying his girlfriend over his shoulder.

For some reason she insisted on dividing her house into two separate parts. The variety acts were assigned quarters on one side of the hall and the straight actors on the other. She then did her best to ensure that the two branches of the profession did not meet.

It was here that we first met Dame Flora Robson who, as a well-established and mature actress, took a genuine interest in Eric and me. Although it was frowned on, she often came over to our side of the digs to talk about variety and how well we were doing. She even took the trouble to come along to the Hulme Hippodrome to see us perform – little realising, I suppose, that twenty-odd years on she would be appearing as a star guest in one of our TV shows. When we first invited her onto the show after all those years she was delighted: 'People think I'm dead,' she told us. 'And that can sometimes lose me quite a lot of work.'

The word soon got round about digs which were worth avoiding. There were the coded messages in the visitors' book, of course, but by the time we saw them it was too late. Far better to be warned of places to avoid.

We were lucky by and large, and our stories of dubious digs were confined to the ones we used to tell as part of our act. Like the two performers who buy themselves a bottle of sherry at the beginning of the week and put it on the sideboard in the dining room. As each day goes by they see it slowly emptying and, knowing they haven't had a nip, assume the landlady has been helping herself. To put a stop to this they decide to top it up by peeing into it. As the level drops, so they top it up day by day. When they are about to leave the landlady approaches them and hopes they haven't been upset by her taking liberties with their amontillado: 'But you like your sherry trifle so much that I've been using a drop every night.'

The only real inconvenience we ever encountered was in digs run by landladies who themselves had been in the business. We would come home starving from some rehearsal, sit down at the table and look forward to some home-made food when the landlady would come in and give us edited highlights of her career in variety. After putting up with a ten-minute spot of hers we had only just had the soup. Before we got round to the main course we had to watch her doing the dance routine and going into her big finish. By which time the food was burnt or cold or both.

Landladies were often good for trying out new material. You had to be careful, of course, that you picked the right one. Some of our more suggestive material might not go down too well with the straight-laced. We had one very good bull-fighting routine, for instance, which used to get a lot of laughs, playing on the suggestive use of the totally invented word 'machotte'. It went, with variations, something like this:

Ernie: You're a bullfighter so you must look the part. You wear a three-cornered hat.
Eric: What for?
Ernie: For your three-cornered head.
Eric: What else do I need?
Ernie: You need your machotte.
Eric: My what?
Eric's face by now is getting the laughs.
Ernie: Your machotte. When the bull comes in you whip out your machotte.
Eric: How long is my machotte?
Ernie: Over two feet long. You whip it out and place it between the bull's eyes.
Eric: Won't it bend?
Ernie: No. But wait, who is that up there? It's the President of

the Bull Ring.
Eric: What should I do?
Ernie: With your machotte you cut the ear of the bull and
   present it to him.
Eric: I know what he'll say.
Ernie: What?
Eric: Hello, hello, what's this 'ere?

It got a lot of laughs at the Friday and Saturday houses but
wasn't to be recommended if we were unsure of our audience.
Or our landlady.

*

Talent is easy to spot. As young men sitting in the auditorium
of a provincial theatre watching new acts rehearse we could
tell within a minute who was going to do well and who wasn't.
Even when we watched a row of dancers all doing apparently
the same thing we could always spot the girl who had that bit
extra, that indefinable spark of personality which singled her
out from the rest.

One Monday morning in June 1952 at a band call at the
Empire, Edinburgh the phenomenon occurred again. This
time the star in question was one Joan Bartlett, a tall,
attractive young dancer who made an instant impact on Eric.
Before long they were seeing each other regularly, and before
the year was out they were married.

By this time I had been going out with Doreen for five years,
and although things were pretty serious between us I was
inexplicably slow at tying the knot. At one point I almost lost
her when she considered following a boyfriend of hers to
South Africa where he had a job as a chef. But I must have
been making some impression on her because, after proposing
on Valentine's Day 1952, we were married in January of the
following year.

Doreen often used to tease me about being unromantic.
Apparently she had been very impressed that I had asked if I

might kiss her goodnight on one of our early dates at Lord John Sanger's Circus, but had been continually disappointed that I'd failed to live up to such promise. For a long time she accused me of never writing her love letters but of merely sending her my tour list to arrange meetings when our trains crossed at Preston or Crewe.

The first few weeks of our married life were spent in the converted bus and caravan while Eric and I were finishing a pantomime run in Sheffield. It snowed very hard that winter, and as the bus was by now equipped with a paraffin heater I have fond memories of cosy evenings together with steaming mugs of tea after the evening show was over. We have been inseparable ever since even though our relationship with the Bedford bus was destined to come to a premature end once persistent snow drifts and ice in the engine ensured that it never started again.

We bought ourselves a small house in Doreen's home town of Peterborough, having followed our caravan dwelling with a spell in her parents' spare room. While the house provided a solid base for us and gave us the feeling of domestic and financial security, we were rarely there – more often than not touring together away from home.

Quite soon into their marriage Eric and Joan had children, a fact which obviously complicated their joint travelling. Doreen and I, however, made a conscious decision not to have any children, so that the two of us would not have to spend time apart, with Doreen looking after a baby in Peterborough. Doreen had run a dancing school for a time and although her own touring days as a dancer were over she still enjoyed the excitement of showbusiness life and was happy to continue touring with me.

Home, for us, has been wherever the two of us are together which has meant not only almost forty years of sharing every aspect of each other's lives but also many years of being able to share our home, wherever it is, with others. At Christmas time, for example, when commitment to a pantomime meant that some performers were unable to go home, Doreen used to hold special dinner parties for those in the cast with nowhere to go. If we rented a place during a run we would always hold open house for people to drop in. They were busy, sociable times with pros and their friends filling the house with singing and laughter; there were parties and lots of fun to break up the hard work.

*

Blackpool summer season, when we could get it, was the best of the lot, dispelling the memories of cramped railway compartments, unreliable motor cars and grim-looking digs at a stroke. The season was twelve or fourteen weeks of sheer joy and not a little glamour.

Our first taste of this legendary Northern seaside town, however, was not a complete success, and I remember this period with a mixture of fondness and alarm. We were doing well by night at the Empire, Brixton and beginning to get more success, by day, with our radio work. As a direct result we were booked for the Winter Gardens, Blackpool, a much coveted venue, where we appeared with the singer Alan Jones and Harry Worth.

The sea air didn't agree with Alan Jones, and as a compensation he used to retire with a large bottle of something very potent – from time to time failing to appear on stage altogether. George and Alfred Black, the two very grand impresarios who had booked us, approached Eric and me and told us to be ready to go on if he failed to turn up.

For some this might have been a longed-for opportunity. For us it was terrifying. We had material for a couple of spots but nothing we could stretch to a third spot as top-of-the-bill.

One evening we were sitting in our dressing room after our act listening to Alan on stage. We heard his voice getting cracklier and cracklier and knew that very soon we were going to be ordered to fill the breach. We could hear George Black rushing down the corridor, so in desperation Eric and I stripped down to our underpants. When George barged in to

110

send us on we told him it was impossible, that we weren't anywhere near ready and he would do better to get someone else. At the last minute he managed to get a singer, Eve Boswell, to replace us as replacements for Alan Jones. Our first outing in Blackpool, which should have been so exciting, turned out to be a mixed blessing.

Much later we found ourselves sharing another bill with Alan in Cardiff. He was top-of-the-bill but had been drinking rather heavily before one of his performances and was clearly having trouble with a number of his called 'The Monkey and the Organ Grinder'. Halfway through, the audience began to give him the slow handclap, which succeeded in needling this decidedly combative Welsh entertainer. He stopped his song, stepped forward as if taking on the entire crowd and said, 'I'm Welsh myself. But I tell you this Welsh audience stinks!'

'Bloody hell!' we thought. 'They're surely not going to get us to replace him now.'

We needn't have worried. This time he had gone too far and they brought the curtain down on him. The audience was in uproar. Alan had to be smuggled out of the theatre by the stage door where a menacing crowd was beginning to assemble fully intending to lynch him. We watched from an upstairs window as this extraordinary man made his extraordinary exit.

*

By the mid-Fifties we were beginning to enjoy – although in a modest way – the fruits of fifteen years in the business, and life was treating us quite handsomely. 'Workers' Playtime' on the radio was bringing us to the attention of a wide audience in the North and this, in turn, led to a long run on a BBC revue called 'Variety Fanfare'.

From this we progressed to a radio show of our own, 'You're Only Young Once', inevitably shortened to 'yoyo', which gave us the opportunity to work in conjunction with scriptwriters on a fast-moving programme which went out live on Sunday evenings. This meant travelling down to Manchester from wherever we happened to be on tour and then working on scripts during the afternoon for the evening broadcast at seven. Often the ink had barely had time to dry.

We were now working seven days a week and the future looked promising. Our 'yoyos' were being masterminded by a BBC producer by the name of Johnny Ammonds, the man who was later to produce our TV shows. So far television itself had not approached us. But in 1954 we got our first stab at it – a delirious moment for a couple of 28-year-olds.

Had we known then, however, how disastrously this episode was going to turn out we would have fended it off with a stout barge-pole. The biggest professional opportunity of our lifetime was about to turn into a waking nightmare and to come within an ace of bringing our career to an untimely and permanent end. Within a matter of weeks every variety critic in the land was preparing to don his black cap before sitting back to pen our showbiz obituaries.

6

Two of a Kind

Our first experience of television was all the more nightmarish for being a totally *unexpected* disaster. So far, with the exception of the odd setback when we were just getting started, our career had been a steady, if slow, progression. Doreen and I could afford a house and a car – a Triumph Mayflower, I remember, for which I paid £600 in cash – and from our base in Peterborough we could motor quite conveniently to show dates North and South.

As Eric and I got more successful we were earning more money. Our £35-a-week bookings jumped to £65 and then to £125, and before long we were fetching £200 plus. We were appearing well up on the variety bill and establishing quite a name for ourselves on the pantomime circuit.

On some occasions we were appearing with top-of-the-bill acts who were, quite frankly, not as big as we were. If the top was a singer we were unconcerned; there was no competition. But if he was a comic then there would be that little bit of edge to sharpen our performance. The pecking order was just as fierce as it ever had been. But still we were doing well. We had every expectation of building on this success with a new departure into TV. How wrong we were.

The Light Entertainment department of BBC Television had clearly taken note of what we had been doing on radio. That and a brief TV appearance on a show televised from the Tower Ballroom, Blackpool convinced them that we were potentially bankable television material.

6. Two of a Kind

The Head of Light Entertainment at the time was a man called Ronnie Waldman who had a lot of faith in us as the up-and-coming stars of the small screen. We discussed ideas for the series and were assigned a team of writers to develop some routines. The guest star of the first show was to be the hugely popular singer of the day Alma Cogan.

In retrospect I can see only too clearly where we went wrong. It was a combination of thin material, lack of experience of the medium and over-expectation. We had a couple of reliable 12-minute spots which we could use to great effect in the theatre but which were not immediately suited to the small screen. By the time we had modified them – often with the 'help' of scriptwriters who were unfamiliar with our style – we had, let's say, a couple of strong routines each four or five minutes long. But the show lasted half an hour. And, what was more, we had been signed up for six of them.

What Christ had done with five loaves and two fishes we were being asked to do with our comedy routines. And on the evidence of the finished product we lacked his touch. We simply could not carry the material that long.

There was no backing out, though, as the series, 'Running Wild', was well under way by now. It was scheduled, billed and ready for transmission before we knew where we were, and on 21st April 1954 the public sat down to watch Morecambe and Wise's big excursion into national television.

The next day was worse than even the gloomiest Tuesday morning at the Kardomah. The reviews were the hardest we had ever had. 'How do two commonplace performers such as these get elevated to the position of having a series built around them? This was one of the most embarrassingly unfunny evenings I have spent in front of the screen for some time,' said one.

Others were shorter and straight to the point: 'How dare they put such mediocre talent on television?' and 'Alma Cogan stood out like a flower in a garden of weeds.' But perhaps the most vitriolic was: 'Definition of the week. TV set – the box they buried Morecambe and Wise in.'

114

We were both knocked sideways. Initial shock gave way to depression and a serious reconsideration of our future. The shockwaves were immense – even prompting Sadie to telephone us to ask what the hell was going on.

'I daren't show my face outside the house,' she said, or something very much like it. 'Everybody's talking about it round here. I can't go shopping in Morecambe for fear of who I might see. I think we're going to have to move house.'

Eric became terribly morose, losing all his sparkle for days and threatening to pack in TV for good. He was personally upset by the whole episode, and whenever I went round to see him dejection hung over him like an actual, physical presence.

I used to keep him going on occasions like this, making him laugh, cheering him up, generally encouraging him to look on the optimistic side. True, there was, on the face of it, very little to be optimistic about, but I took the view that we had to keep going rather than allow this setback to get us down.

Eric had a tendency to take things far more personally than I did. It was an endearing trait, but its disadvantage was that it caused him a lot of stress. Despite what the public saw of him he was a very insecure person at heart.

It came out in the most trivial of ways at times. He never liked driving, for instance, and when he was persuaded to take the car anywhere he would get in a panic about where he was going to park. He used to worry a lot. His mother had been a great influence on him, fending for him, looking after him and planning things out for him. Now he was married and had a child I think responsibility was coming home to him at last. And he worried about it.

The bad reception of 'Running Wild' was not calculated to boost his confidence (nor mine, of course, but I had a harder shell), and the two of us tried in vain to have the series taken off prematurely. Ronnie Waldman insisted we see it through and, assuring us we really did have a great future in television, nursed us through the remaining five shows.

*

115

Six weeks later, bashed and bruised, we found ourselves back in what we knew to be our true element, variety theatre, where, surprisingly, our temporary (if sensational) failure had done nothing to blunt our reception. On the contrary, managers were able to use our TV status to boost our names. In fact, although critics, impresarios, and those in the business had been avidly watching the show, most ordinary folk had not, since there were very few people on the circuit we worked who owned a television set.

TV still had an indefinable allure, though, and the mere mention of 'TV stars Morecambe and Wise', or 'TV comedians', proved to be an extra draw at the box office. The management put us low down on the bill of the Ardwick Hippodrome in Manchester after the series came to an end, but the audience loved us.

The next few years continued in much the same vein as they had done up to now – with the variety and pantomime work restoring our confidence sufficiently for us to try our hand again at the odd TV appearance. No question of a series this time, of course: we had learnt our lesson. But the occasional comedy routine on a variety bill televised from, say, the London Palladium or the Hackney Empire presented us with no real terrors.

It was the time when Lew Grade, father of ATV and presiding theatrical tycoon of the day, was bringing first-class American acts over here to top the bill and, at his invitation, we found ourselves appearing on stage with people like Lena Horne and Paul Robeson.

By this time we had, with some regret, changed agents. Frank Pope had served us well over the years, but the days of live variety, in which Frank excelled, were numbered. Theatres were closing in response to the unequal challenge of television. We had to move with the times and, despite our unhappy experience of TV so far, we had come to terms with an inescapable reality: continuing success in the business meant success on the box.

That reality came complete with pitfalls, of course. No

longer could we recycle the same material over and over
again. Whereas a variety audience changed nightly from
Glasgow to Plymouth and at all stops in between, a television
audience on any one evening was the sum total of all those
nightly, provincial audiences combined into one. Each time we
performed on television we needed a new routine to satisfy an
incessant and increasing hunger. Take a routine like this:

Ernie: You used to be a boxer didn't you?
Eric: Yes.
Ernie: Were you any good?
Eric: Well, I spent so much time on the canvas they put
    handles on my trunks.
Ernie: Where you popular?
Eric: Yes, they used to sell advertising space on the soles of
    my feet.
Ernie: What were your tactics?
Eric: First a left cross, then a right cross, and usually the Red
    Cross.

Cross-talk like that could be incorporated frequently into a
three-week tour. On TV its shelf life was limited to one
evening and the next appearance demanded more material to
replace it. We couldn't break into this world unaided, so we set
about finding an experienced agent to do it for us. The man we
had chosen to steer us into this new medium was Billy Marsh,
and we relied on his steady helmsmanship from that moment
on.

He engineered our appearances on the small screen with
exactly the right blend of persistence and reserve, not
over-exposing us prematurely but ensuring that we popped up
with well-judged frequency on such show-case programmes as
'Sunday Night at the London Palladium' in comedy spots
which perfectly suited our routine. We were beginning to get
noticed.

*

117

So it was that in the summer of 1961 when we were appearing in variety in Torquay, we received a telephone call from Billy asking us if we would be interested in signing up for a 13-week television series for ATV to be broadcast live in the autumn.

It was risky. And neither Eric nor I relished the prospect of experiencing the sort of depression which might follow a second failure. Added to that was the knowledge that a second failure would be the finish of us. We talked it over and decided to accept only if we could be guaranteed the scriptwriters of our choice, writers whose work we could depend on. There was a period of humming and hawing at ATV, but eventually they agreed.

Dick Hills and Sid Green were the writers we had in mind, two former schoolteachers whose scripts for various comedians of the day we had consistently admired. 'Sid and Dick' were duly recruited and we began to rehearse.

The relationship between writer and performer is a complex one since both bring complementary skills to the final product and both are egotistical enough to want to claim the credit. The writers are the wordsmiths, great at conjuring up abstract ideas and writing gags to suit them. The performers are the practitioners, experienced entertainers who know instinctively whether the ideas (which may be hilarious in rehearsal) will work in practice.

At the start of every working day the three of us would assemble promptly at ten o'clock. The three of us, please note – Sid invariably arrived at least half an hour after the rest owing to what he habitually referred to as 'a touch of the domestics'. Then we would run through a number of ideas that Sid and Dick had come up with, try them out, improvise some dialogue or simply read the script that the writers had produced.

Eric and I would offer ideas of our own, mentally opening drawers to rummage around twenty years' worth of stored material, and between us would arrive at a string of gags which secretaries would write down as we spoke. Half-way

118

through the day the material would be readjusted and polished to give us, if we were lucky, a routine which we could rehearse, commit to memory, and produce for the live programme.

The process of creation, then, was a shared one, full of laughs and good humour but not without its tensions. For one thing there was the unstated tendency (at moments of extreme agitation it was stated only too clearly!) to claim the credit for a gag that went well and to shuffle off the responsibility for one that flopped.

In other words Sid and Dick might say, 'Look, we wrote a perfectly funny gag which got lots of laughs in rehearsal but you ruined it by doing such and such a thing'. We would counter that by saying, 'It was only thanks to us that the gag managed to raise a smile. It was a weak idea in the first place which we managed to rescue by delivering it in such and such a way.' Mutual recrimination was frequent but short-lived.

Sid and Dick were very talented guys – better educated than the pair of us and a bit older, too – who were good not only with the jokes but also with a lot of the stage business. Sid in particular, I thought, was exceptional at comedy – but occasionally sarcastic with it. Many a time he would wander in, late, after the two of us had been rehearsing with Dick, and sit himself down opposite us with an immediate critique of what was going on.

'No, no. Hopeless,' he would say. 'So and so would have done it much better.'

Since we had been hard at it for an hour or more before he had even deigned to show his face, it isn't difficult to imagine how a remark like that was likely to go down. His sarcasm went down particularly badly with Eric, who on occasions could have a sharp tongue himself. It was usually left to me to smooth things over between them before we continued. 'Constipated Sid', as Eric dubbed him, soon came round, as did Eric himself whose feathers had been harmlessly ruffled by what was an inevitable part of the process of putting together a show.

*

6. *Two of a Kind*

By October the first of the new series was ready and, to the
theme tune of 'Two of a Kind' – a song which became one of our
anthems – the pair of us stepped under the television lights for
a second time with our fingers firmly crossed. The reception
was only lukewarm, and after the first show the familiar cycle
of testy recrimination got under way.

To take an example. We felt that there were simply too many
people on the set for one of the sketches – a spy sketch – to work
effectively. Sid and Dick disagreed and proceeded to write us
similar routines which again were, in our view, overloaded
with comic business and merely swamped the jokes.

As things turned out, though, there was an Equity strike
that week jeopardising the show and, indeed, the whole series.
Eric and I were fortunate in belonging to a different union, the
VAF or Variety Artists' Federation, and so while *we* could take
the stage the small army of extras (all Equity members) could
not. A much reduced cast (in the form of Sid and Dick!) replaced
them.

The result was more economy in the comedy and tighter
focus on us, the performers. It went down well and for the rest
of the run the strike made us conform to the same pattern. Sid
and Dick were forced to concede that we had now hit on a
successful formula which we kept for a further two series to the
apparent satisfaction of management and audience alike.

The shows were fairly traditional in format but contained
the germs of ideas we would go on to develop in what I shall
grandly call 'our mature period'. We opened cold – with no
build-up or introduction – with an attention-grabbing sketch.

For instance, Eric would come forward as a Dixon-of-Dock-
Green-type bobby and look straight at the camera saying how
quiet his beat was, how rarely anything serious happened on
his patch etc etc. While all this was being delivered the camera
pulled back to reveal chaos – banks being robbed, cars being
stolen, fights and total mayhem. Eric, meanwhile, would continue his slow patrol oblivious to it all.

The key lay both in the situation and in the character of the
policeman up front. Gesture and tone were all, and even today I

can see Eric bringing to an essentially simple idea a great richness.

Another opener relied on copying the opening titles of a very popular TV detective series of the day entitled 'The Four Just Men'. The introductory sequence of each weekly episode began portentously with four men swearing allegiance to each other in the fight against crime and sealing their mutual bond with their signature in a book which was passed from one to the other to the accompaniment of solemn music. Our version involved – who else? – Sid, Dick, Eric and me.

The music begins, the book appears. First Sid signs. Then he ritually passes the book to Dick. Expressionless, he adds his name and passes the book to Eric. The solemn music continues as Eric begins to sign. Halfway through he has a problem with his pen and scratches and shakes it in a way totally out of keeping with the music. As the camera pans to me, the fourth member about to sign, it reveals an equally solemn figure covered in ink blots from Eric's pen. This turned out to be a very successful visual gag which kick-started the show into life.

After the opening routine we had a trad. jazz band of the Kenny Ball, Chris Barber variety followed by a guest singer – perhaps our old friends Pearl Carr and Teddy Johnson – and a comedy sketch. After the break we had perhaps another, longer sketch followed by a second number from the guest and our closing spot. The closing was usually a lengthier routine enlivened always by a running gag which gave the series continuity and stamped on it something of our personal identity.

'Home from the Wars' was the broad title given to a final bit of business involving Eric repeatedly being denied the chance to get into bed with the girl – supposed to be his wife – after he had been away in the wars. We put him in a suit of armour, for example, whose visor clamped shut just as he was about to kiss the girl. His muffled cries of protest were guaranteed to get lots of laughs.

Another routine relied on promising Eric, early on in the show, that he would get the chance to do a show-stopping finale: Abraham Lincoln giving his Gettysburg Address, Quasimodo going through a Hunchback of Notre Dame scene, or Fagin teaching Oliver Twist how to pick pockets. When we came to the closing moments Eric would be half made up and ready to do his bit only to be told by me that the time had run out and we would have to do the song, 'Two of a Kind' to finish.

Once again the comedy relied on a non-verbal relationship between the two of us: on our taking what was a good but lifeless idea on paper and transforming it into a flesh-and-blood situation which produced the right mixture of expectation and disappointment. Whether people saw it like that I very much doubt, but the main thing was they were laughing. The next thing was that we were invited onto a Royal Command Performance.

*

In some ways this turned out to be the break that never was. It was 1961 at the London Palladium with Bruce Forsyth top-of-the-bill and in the audience, unknown to us, one of the most influential men in American television, Ed Sullivan. He liked us and booked us straightaway at $5,000 a shot for a show that attracted an audience of millions. The drawback – for Eric more than for me – was that it was an audience of millions of *Americans* who took a bit of time to warm to an English act.

We were flown over, housed in style and engaged to do three spots on his weekly show. We started out with high hopes but ended coming down to earth with a bumpy landing. It was probably the only time I became impatient with Eric.

Ed Sullivan was charm itself, a genial, expansive organiser who knew the variety field inside out and who prided himself on being a performer too. In all honesty I would have to rate his performing skills rather lower than his entrepreneurial know-how. He introduced us first as a threesome – 'Ladies and Gentlemen, will you welcome Morrey, Camby and Wise' and then looked off stage expectantly for the third member to appear. The second time he introduced us as 'Morton and

White' and even, in one bizarre configuration, as 'Bartholomew and Wisdom'.

Our spots were done live in front of an audience but recorded and included in the following week's show. Starting off the routine cold was hard-going, but it could have been worse and we certainly got some good laughs. Much of the material had to be adjusted to suit what we were told was the 'Bible Belt' audience. The remotest reference, no matter how oblique, to anything which might just possibly be construed as 'immoral' was cut. No questions asked. Or, at least, no explanations given.

So a long-standing musical routine which involved Eric filling in with 'Rum-titty-tum-tum' was given the blue pencil treatment on the grounds of its overtly racy reference. What reference, for goodness sake? We were not even aware of any dubious connotation and suggested, in vain, that the immorality was in the ear of the listener. No luck. It became 'Dum-diddy-dum-dum'. Nobody was taking any chances.

At the time we used the word 'it' in a deliberately self-conscious way. We gave it two meanings but kept it strictly within the bounds of what we considered good taste. It wasn't sufficient for the Americans.

For example, we had a ventriloquism routine with a standard evening-suited dummy sitting on Eric's lap. I came up to him and said, 'I never knew you were a ventriloquist. I didn't think you were interested in it.'

To which Eric replied, 'I'm not any more. I'm too old. That's why I took this up.'

Too risqué. The joke was cut. As also was another which began with me putting my arm round Eric and saying, 'I've got a great idea.'

'I bet you have,' said Eric, 'I've heard about you.'

It was out: 'No, guys, it won't work. It's too sort of fagotty. You know what I mean?'

Well, yes, we did know what he meant, but that was the point. And we were hardly laying it on thick. Anyway, our whole act went through numerous changes but, in my opinion, if not in Eric's, it still worked – just.

But it wasn't enough for Eric. He was unhappy with the reception we got, unhappy that the applause wasn't overwhelming, unhappy, I think, because he didn't *feel* he was being funny enough. OK, we might have had to reshape the routine here and there but eventually, I still believe to this day, we could have cracked it in America.

As it was, Eric hated it. So much so that after every programme we caught the first available plane home. We did the show on Sunday night and – it is hard to believe now – caught a return flight at something like 11.30 pm. Eric was so keen to leave. Why?

I have often wondered and I have come up with only a partial explanation which had something to do with his basic insecurity. On stage there wasn't a hint of it. I had total confidence that, whatever happened, Eric could take control of it and use it, with the most superb sense of timing, for his own purposes. Anyone who ever appeared with him on stage – and this applied to all the stars who worked with us later – need not have feared. They were in the safest pair of hands imaginable. And yet off stage, at times like the Ed Sullivan episode, he seemed to go to pieces.

He didn't like *not* getting the laughs. He didn't like walking the streets of New York – which he hated anyway – and *not* being recognised. In England we were already household names and he only had to open his mouth or look at the camera to have an audience in the palm of his hand. In America all that was absent and he didn't take to it well. He needed the recognition. Needed to be told he was funny.

I tried to encourage him, but the encouragement had no effect. To this day I am convinced we could have made it in America. It was a disappointment to me at the time and a frustration of a long-standing ambition to 'get to Hollywood', which, though dating back to the Nignog revues and the club dates with Dad, had never left me. It is, of course, highly likely that we would never have made it to Hollywood anyway, but in 1961 I was willing to give it a try. I was willing to work at it.

6. Two of a Kind

Ed Sullivan was very kind to us. He took us out for meals, introduced us to lots of theatre people and treated us like star material. He even joined in a routine of ours which became one of our standing sig-tunes – Boom, ooh, ya, ta, ta, Tah! The idea, like the Woody Woodpecker song, was for me to sing 'Are you Lonesome Tonight' while Eric sang a rhythmic refrain 'Boom, ooh, ya, ta, ta, Tah!' Ed was assigned the 'boom' and, try as he might, bless him, he never got it right.

The American episode ended without bitterness but with the lurking feeling, on my part at least, that this was unfinished business.

The final show was in 1968 at a special gala salute to mark the 80th birthday of Irving Berlin. It was a glittering occasion, introduced by the President of the United States, Lyndon B. Johnson, with Bob Hope and Bing Crosby in the line-up. We were thrilled to be included in such distinguished company. Less thrilled the morning after to read a review in the New York *Daily News Record* which read '... there was one curiously out of place vaudeville team called Morecambe and Wise which should remain England's problem, not ours'. There was, we reflected philosophically as we packed our bags, no answer to that.

One of the more curious phenomena to stand out from our farewell evening was the spectacle of Bing Crosby singing 'White Christmas'. Nothing very unusual about that. Except that he was singing it with idiot boards off stage to help him remember the words of a song he must have sung a thousand times and more!

*

Back in England lives and careers resumed their normal course after this temporary but tantalising diversion. We were working terrifically hard at ATV and combining it with variety, pantomime and summer season. We were very hungry in those days, doing everything which was offered to us and daring to turn down nothing. It became a compulsion, an unhealthy

125

pursuit of money or fame or something. But, like a powerful addiction, success could not be resisted.

People were making demands on us constantly. When not performing we were asked to open a fête, attend a dinner, give a speech, judge a competition, award a prize ... the list was endless. For Doreen and me things were marginally easier because we travelled everywhere together. For Eric life was hard since to the sheer pressure of work was added the strain of being away from his home and family.

Then came the films. These should have turned out to be pleasant, leisurely interludes in our careers, breaks from the predictable round of TV, variety and pantomime, and permanent records of our comic achievements. Sadly, they were none of these things. In 1964 we had high expectations that we were about to make it in films – an ambition both of us had for a long time nursed – but the deal we struck for three consecutive films didn't allow us to give of our best.

As a result *The Intelligence Men, That Riviera Touch* and *The Magnificent Two* were disappointing and received only adverse critical acclaim. The scripts were poor, the budget was low and, to take our share of the blame, the medium didn't really suit us. For a start we did not have an audience, and our best work was done when we had somebody in front of us to react to. Secondly, and crucially, the filming process involved constant retakes from different angles of the same scene.

Now, our comedy business relied on a very close relationship between the two of us – a remark from me provoked an instant reaction from Eric. Once that remark was made Eric's gesture or look or tone was lost for good and it wasn't always possible to recreate it a second time for the sake of a new camera shot. As a result, our routines weren't as slick as we would have hoped and, to cut short what was a rather more complex series of reasons, the three films weren't much good.

We had half hoped to do more films – the next time on our own terms – but very shortly Eric was to have his first heart attack, which was effectively to rule out that tempting possibility. The people in the film business weren't prepared to stake those enormous sums of money on an enterprise which might flounder because one of the stars falls ill. This, then, was to be the end of our cinema career, although we later did a TV film for Thames called *Night Train to Murder*.

The disappointment soon wore off as we concentrated our energy on theatre and TV. The work schedule was frenetic. Pantomime in Birmingham or Manchester, summer season in Blackpool or Bournemouth, television, commercials, personal appearances – on many occasions we were working seven days a week, and when we weren't working we were travelling.

But we couldn't stop because we were in such huge demand and, mindful that there might come a time when we were in less demand, we capitalised on our increasing popularity. We were voted Light Entertainment Personalities of the Year; we were honoured by the Variety Club of Great Britain; we were invited on to Royal Variety Performances; and we broke box office records at a number of theatres we played. It seemed that we could do no wrong.

From time to time, however, the pressure of the workload became evident to both of us. Eric was smoking heavily, for instance: over sixty cigarettes a day and sometimes as many as a hundred. We came off stage exhausted and dripping with perspiration, collapsed in chairs in the dressing room sometimes too tired to stand, and had no time in between bookings to replenish our reserves of energy.

On one celebrated date at the London Palladium the tiredness was very nearly our undoing. It was in 1965 and we were topping the bill. Our act the previous evening had not gone terribly well with technical hitches dulling the edge of some of the sketches. We were tired, of course, and not performing at full strength so our routine was not rapturously received.

As we were about to take the stage Eric remarked that he hoped the audience was going to be better than last night's. It was the sort of casual remark, uttered in the wings, that we had been making for the past thirty years in the business. The difference on this occasion was that it was picked up by the radio microphones we were wearing and relayed to the entire

127

audience. We thus succeeded in exhausting all our credit with them at a stroke, and not only did we come on to muted applause but we went off to it as well. There was worse to come.

As the curtain closed and we made our exit Eric made another remark, again forgetting that the audience was going to pick it up loud and clear.

'That was the worst bloody act we've ever done,' he said.

To which the audience, as one, muttered, 'Yes.'

However, we ignored all the warning signs and worked on, stretching ourselves to the limit. In addition to the ATV series we were doing a show called 'Piccadilly Palace'. This was another Lew Grade production but made with an American audience in mind and exported across the Atlantic. In addition we were also booked for a summer season at Yarmouth.

*

It was at about this time, early in 1968, that we fell out with Lew Grade and left ATV. A number of reasons prompted our decision. First, we had been offered £39,000 for a three-year contract tying us to thirteen shows a year. It was a lot of money (though in my view, not enough) and Eric was convinced we should take it.

I disagreed. My view was that three years was too long a commitment. Thirty-nine shows needed a lot of material and if, for one reason or another, we couldn't come up with it we would be in deep trouble. Far better to take it a year at a time and be sure of being able to maintain standards.

Not only that, I was, and am, a big believer in professional freedom, and the big danger in our business is that an artist can get locked into exclusive contracts which prevent him from developing in other ways. He must be able to sell his wares in the market place and be available, if opportunities come along, to take them. As usual, Eric left me to do the haggling.

6. Two of a Kind

In the first instance, then, we fell out over money. In fact, in Lew Grade's memoirs he actually complained about how difficult I was to do business with. A number of times we had him shouting at us, 'Why do you boys want all this money?'

My answer was simple. We all wanted the money. And if he wanted it, so did we. Eric, of course, let me do the talking. In a sense I was rather flattered that the great Lord Grade, a consummate businessman himself, should pick me out as a tough negotiator.

Our main point of conflict, though, was that he intended to shoot the next series in black-and-white whereas we felt that colour was more appropriate. He wasn't having any of it. We refused point blank to do it in black-and-white, to which he replied to the effect that we would do as we were told. It wasn't a tactic guaranteed to go down well with us.

We had never liked being told what to do. All through our careers we had been prepared to starve rather than be bossed around. As self-employed performers we had only our talent and our freedom to call our own. The talent looked after itself. Sure, we worked at it; but essentially we either had it or we didn't. Freedom was another matter. Over that we had complete control and surrendering it was fraught with hazard.

We couldn't be bullied into a deal. People could lead us by the nose, they could kid us, cajole us and flatter us but we couldn't be pushed. The colour/black-and-white argument was not resolved, so we took the decision – a momentous one and risky, but ultimately the right one – to part company with ATV.

We ended our fruitful collaboration with a furious row. For a time we feared this might be our abiding memory of a once happy partnership, but fortunately Lew himself had no desire to see things end in bitterness either, and he was gracious enough to send us each a box of his famous cigars once he (and we) had cooled down a little.

*

6. Two of a Kind

We were lucky enough, however, to get an immediate offer from the BBC in the form of Bill Cotton, then Head of Light Entertainment at BBC Television. He agreed to shoot the new series in colour, and it was scheduled for summer broadcast on BBC2. We took our two scriptwriters, Sid and Dick, with us and so, although working for another outfit, we could maintain the continuity. The shows went down well, giving us nationwide exposure, which only increased our drawing power at the theatres and clubs throughout the country.

It was during this promising phase of our TV career that sadness struck. On the 18th February 1966, as we were rehearsing in London, news came that my father had died. Although I had known of his illness for some time I was not fully prepared for the shock. But we were deep in rehearsals and I simply could not let the grief take hold. There were schedules to meet, studios to use, routines to perfect; there were responsibilities to meet. Such is the reality behind the time-worn phrase 'the show must go on'.

I took one day off to return to Leeds to pay a final farewell. The guiding light of my life had gone out, but its afterglow still remains. Even now I can feel the presence of Dad inside me. That optimism, that sunny personality; always there to inspire me. I came back to London subdued but philosophical. Dad would have understood. He would have known instinctively of the pressures we were under and I'm sure he would have been proud that by now the two of us were in big demand.

So much in demand, I am tempted to boast, that we were once summoned to Windsor Castle for an unpublicised appearance in front of the Royal Family. We got a call via a third (or fifth or tenth) party to take part in a variety entertainment specially organised for the Queen and her close entourage. They don't have a special theatre for this sort of thing – more a cabaret arrangement with a platform at one end of a reception room.

It was here, much later, that I was told by none other than His Royal Highness the Duke of Edinburgh that, at the height of our success, the Royal Family would delay Christmas dinner until the Morecambe and Wise show was over, and it was here that the Queen Mother asked Eric how he did his trick 'with the paper bag'.

The trick with the paper bag was a running gag of his. He held an empty bag in front of him, pretended to throw something up in the air and to catch it in the bag. By flicking the bag between forefinger and thumb he managed to make it seem that something had actually landed in the bag. It was a very juvenile (but very popular) bit of business, and what struck me about the Queen Mother's curiosity was not the curiosity itself so much as the possibility that she might intend to use it as an impromptu entertainment for visiting heads of state.

Protocol prevented me from enquiring too closely as to whether the information was for her personal use alone or whether she intended to pull this gag out of the hat on ceremonial occasions to break the ice.

*

In 1968 we seemed to have everything: financial and material success, popular and critical acclaim, and respect from within the profession itself. The two of us, starting out from unpromising circumstances, had negotiated a course through the shifting currents of the pre- and post-war entertainment scene, had caught the television wave at just the right moment, and had been carried by it, intact, to arrive on the long-promised shores of personal and professional fulfilment. Then the hurricane struck.

131

TOM ARNOLD and JOHN BEAUMONT present

THE
SLEEPING   BEAUTY

Book by Phil Park and David Croft
Songs by Phil Park, David Croft and Cyril Ornadel
Costumes Designed and Executed by R. St. John Roper
Decor by Edward Delany and Tod Kingman

Produced by LOUIS BARBER

Choreography by MAUREEN ROBINS

Characters in order of appearance :

Florizel, Guardian of Fairyland .... BETTY EMERY

Caribosse, a Witch .... DOROTHY DAMPIER

Court Chamberlain .... JAMES HINSON

Princess Melanie .... PATRICIA LAMBERT

The Queen, her Mother .... TONY HEATON

The King, her Father .... ERIC MORECAMBE

Presto, the Jester .... ERNIE WISE

The Sergeant of the Guard .... CHARLES HARRIS

The Ambassador .... JOHNNIE JOHNSON

Prince Michael, from the New World
DAVID   WHITFIELD
The Great Wizard .... CHARLES HARRIS

JEAN PEARCE CHILDREN

THE GRAND DANCERS AND SINGERS

Pantomime programme, 1961–62

7

Hurricane in Batley

With a comic inappropriateness that wasn't lost on Eric himself, the site preordained for his date with destiny was Jimmy Corrigan's Variety Club, Batley, West Yorkshire.

This wasn't normally the type of venue we liked playing. Clubs were never our favourite spots because we couldn't be sure of the audience's full attention. There was always a bit of background noise, people ordering drinks or chatting at the bar, which put us off our stride and didn't bring out the best in us.

Many a time in clubs we were performing to people who were half drunk, to be honest, or certainly quite merry, which rarely made for the greatest stability in an audience. We never touched so called 'blue' material, so an audience of late-night drinkers didn't always take to our act. In some clubs performers were even known to have had beer thrown over them. We certainly had managed to avoid that in our time but even on the best of occasions the atmosphere didn't suit me.

I hated having to leave the hotel at 9 pm to do a show at 11 or later. I hated having to enter by the kitchen door to make my way to the dressing room. At least we were able to insist that no drinks were served during our act, but looking over a sea of tables stacked high with bottles had a rather deadening effect. We were always happier in theatres rather than clubs.

Jimmy Corrigan's, however, was different. Sure, it was a great barn of a place with the usual, slightly distracting bar at

133

the rear of the auditorium, but it was a very prestigious Northern venue. Jimmy paid very good money to attract the best stars of the day to his part of the world and, lured by the certainty of an appreciative audience, the stars duly came. This, in turn, generated a momentum of its own, and before long most comics and singers had Jimmy's Variety Club firmly pencilled in their touring diary.

We were booked to appear in November 1968 at a fee for a week's work of something like £4,000, which was itself a powerful inducement to travel North when we already had a more than full schedule. We started at midnight intending to do an hour and a quarter. As we were coming up to the hour Eric whispered to me that he did not feel too well and that we should cut it short.

As he told me much later, he was in quite a lot of pain and, indeed, I could see from the look on his face that something was the matter. I had no idea, nor did he, that he was actually having the heart attack there and then on stage before a packed house. Looking back at it, I can only gasp in admiration at him for keeping the act going for as long as he did.

Backstage he told me to deal with the autographs and then he set off for his hotel saying he would be feeling better by the morning. The details of that eventful journey were made, by Eric, into a classic comedy saga which stood comparison with the best in situation comedy.

It was just after one in the morning when he got into his car, one of the latest Jensen models with all the luxuries, like automatic gears and power steering. After a few minutes the pains in his chest and back began to become more severe and he was having great difficulty driving. By this time he realised he had better try to find a hospital but, as a stranger in Leeds, he was totally lost and unable, so late in the evening, to find a living soul for directions. Eventually he spotted a young man walking home and asked him if he could direct him to the hospital. It was the classically infuriating scenario.

'You take the first left here, then go up the hill turn right at the lights – no, left – then round a one-way system. Stay in the left lane – is it the left lane? – yes, the left lane and turn sharp right after that. Now you've got to be careful to avoid ...' and so it went on.

Eric was in no condition to take it all in so he asked the man to take the wheel and drive him there. But of all the people to choose Eric had hit on an ex-Army man whose experience of driving was confined to tanks. With kangaroo starts from traffic lights and emergency stops at junctions, Eric was knocked from side to side in the car until he eventually arrived at the hospital only to be told that they didn't accept emergency cases.

Lurching off once again, the two men engaged in a one-sided conversation about show business and how exciting it must be to travel the country.

'Oh, and how did that joke of yours go? You know, the one with the ventriloquist's dummy.'

It was difficult to persuade the man that a comedian's thoughts, in what he thinks may be his final moments on the planet, are not automatically taken up with a hilarious review of his funniest moments on screen.

As they arrived at Leeds Infirmary a stretcher was brought out and Eric was put on it, only to be faced with a scrap of paper, a pen and a request for an autograph 'before you go'.

The story continued with countless surreal elaborations dreamed up by Eric each time he retold it. Like the time he was taken to the operating theatre and the surgeon decided to dispense with the anaesthetic. Instead he pulled out an LP of Des O'Connor hits, put it on the turntable and Eric was out for the count. Or the time Des informed his audience one evening that Eric was ill and asked them all to pray for his recovery – every one of them. Eric told him later that 'those fifteen people there made all the difference'.

*

Such humour was not, of course, in great evidence on the night itself when I received a call around two o'clock informing me that my partner of half a lifetime had just had a heart attack and was critically ill in intensive care.

I made my way to Eric's hotel to collect his things and stared down glumly at his shoes, reasoning in the forlorn state that engulfed me that it could be some time before Eric was dancing in them again, if ever.

Doreen and I were staying a few miles away from his hotel – much to the surprise of people who always assumed that we shared the same hotel and generally lived in each other's pockets when not on stage. When I had collected her the two of us drove with mounting foreboding to the hospital to find Eric sitting up in bed, deeply suntanned after a recent holiday, and apparently in the peak of health.

A heart monitor by the bedside seemed tame enough, and Eric by now was up to exchanging characteristic wisecracks with doctors and nurses who came in intermittently to check on his progress.

The prognosis was cautious but hopeful. It had been a comparatively severe heart attack but was unlikely to prevent him leading a normal life in the future providing he looked after himself reasonably well, cutting down on his cigarettes and stepping down his work schedule a notch or two. Above all a period of three months' rest and convalescence was ordered, during which time there would be no question of getting back on the stage.

Eric was interested to learn (and not unamused by the irony of the timing) that I had just that week cancelled an insurance policy on him. My accountant, concerned that our income would dry up if anything happened to one of us, had suggested I take out a policy which for a modest sum per year would guarantee me reasonable earnings if ever Eric was out of action for a time. Since our act was going from strength to strength and Eric showed no signs of flagging, Doreen and I had decided it was pointless to pay money into the policy. Almost as soon as I had cancelled it Eric, with what can only be called superb comic timing, had his heart attack.

*

7. Hurricane in Batley

Money was going to be less of a problem for me than inactivity. We had savings enough to see us through the convalescence, and the first three months were a real relaxation. Doreen and I had time to spend at home, to visit friends at weekends, to be in one place for long enough not to have to think of the next show date on tour. When Eric decided (wisely) to extend the three months into six I became distinctly underemployed and impatient to get back into the business.

One of the most difficult times was the period just after he had been taken ill when I was forced to deal with the question, repeated hundreds and hundreds of times by well-wishers, 'How is Eric?' The pain of replying gave way to sheer exasperation at having to go through the same rehearsed answer (especially to the press).

When Eric started to get better I took to wearing a badge on my lapel whenever I attended functions. It read: 'Eric's getting much better', to which I added a PS: 'I don't feel so good though.'

The BBC was very reasonable and Bill Cotton was very kind. We had done one successful series for them before the heart attack, and the Light Entertainment Department was happy to wait until Eric was fully recovered before resuming where we had left off. The enforced rest made us reconsider the pattern of our joint working career and led us inevitably to conclude that things couldn't be as hectic as before. We decided to concentrate on the TV work and let theatre appearances take a permanent back seat.

As the television series became more popular we were allowed greater control of the rehearsal time leading up to each programme. We could concentrate more of our attention on the shows without having to worry about squeezing in a summer season here or a pantomime there. However, we felt we couldn't confine ourselves solely to television for financial reasons, and for professional reasons we wanted at least to keep our hand in with a live theatre audience.

As a result I devised a schedule of so-called 'bank raids' which involved a couple of variety bookings at the beginning of rehearsal time, when the pace was less frenetic. In practice we chose a big theatre, went in on a Friday or Saturday, did a couple of shows and then took the money and ran.

Such activity was, however, a good six months off, and in the meantime, apart from press interviews, the odd chat show appearance and so on, the two of us were effectively off the scene. The enforced rest was beneficial, putting an end to the nervous tension that had been affecting me when our work routine was at its most severe. How many times had I woken up with my neck and shoulders locked so stiff with tension that I was unable to turn my head? That, at least, had disappeared.

On the negative side, though, we were faced with a professional disappointment which for a time threatened to be catastrophic.

I got news of this unwelcome development in the most casual way imaginable. Doreen and I had flown to New York in an attempt to persuade Ed Sullivan to screen some of our shows, and after a stop-over in the city we decided to take a short holiday in Barbados as we had sometimes done when Eric and I had been appearing on his show.

An hour into the flight the steward approached me and asked if it was true that Hills and Green were no longer writing for us. I was speechless. If it was true, it was the first I had heard of it. The steward had read in the papers that Sid and Dick had left us to go back to ATV and he now wondered what we were going to do.

So did I. I immediately contacted Eric from Barbados and he, too, was in the dark. In retrospect we should perhaps have realised that six months' idleness would not be welcomed by a pair of writers who needed to earn their bread and butter. But the fact that we were the last to know of their departure struck us as odd and unfair.

Dick was the genial member of the team, an amiable, round and smiling figure we nicknamed 'Father Christmas'. It was left to him to write to us explaining their exclusive contract to ATV which effectively prevented them from ever working with us again. It was a sad and abrupt end to a partnership –

but there we are. That, as they say, is showbusiness.

*

By now Eric was back on his feet again, ready to start working on the new series, but we had a problem. No writers. The BBC was very strong on production and gave us all the backing we needed. It we wanted a big orchestra for a big musical number, we got a big orchestra. If we wanted an elaborate set and complicated props, we got them. The stage hands, the engineers, the sound and lighting men were excellent, but we needed the writers if we were going to have a show at all.

It was in the lift at Television Centre that Bill Cotton solved the problem for us. We had signed a contract for thirteen shows a year for three years. He was taking a significant risk with us because Eric was still not at full strength, but it was a measure of the faith he had in us as performers that he was prepared to book us for that long. Not only that, he guaranteed us a three-week rehearsal period and a two-day recording schedule for each show. It was a generous arrangement which enabled Eric to work at a pace which would not be positively life-threatening and the two of us jointly to give our energies to producing a first-rate show which would bear all the marks of a product on which time and care had been lavished.

'We've got over the problem with the writers, too,' said Bill Cotton in the lift. 'What do you say to Eddie Braben?'

It seemed to me to be an excellent choice. He had been writing for Ken Dodd for some time, giving him material which we had admired, and now he was free to work with us. A meeting was arranged and we were introduced to a tall, bluff Liverpudlian who immediately told us, 'I don't do sketches. I can only write jokes.'

To which our reply was, 'If you can give us six good jokes a show we can do the rest.'

As things turned out his assessment of his own contribution was an oversimplification. He was the man behind the 'star' format whereby we invited a famous personality onto the show

139

each week, he devised my character as the third-rate playwright constantly boasting of the 'plays wot I wrote', and he it was who had the sure touch of drawing up a series of catch lines which became both running gags and personal trade marks in our routines.

Some, like 'You can't see the join', dated way back to the days when we were making our way in variety and sharing digs in Chiswick with an American acrobat called Paul Kafka, who wore a very obvious top-piece to conceal a bald spot.

The toupée, or rug, as it was universally known in the theatrical profession, had severe defects. First, its colour, which provided a bold contrast with his real hair; secondly, its texture which, of the finest Axminster, seemed strangely thicker than his wispy side pieces; and thirdly, its fit which lent him the look of a Chippendale in a car seat cover.

In short, when Paul came down for breakfast he gave every impression of wearing a slumbering otter on his head. Hence Eric's and my gasps of feigned admiration to each other and our ironic comment on the invisibility of the join. At this point let me make it quite clear, if only for vanity's sake, that my hair is my own. Long years of experience have turned it white but at least I can claim legitimate ownership.

Other catch lines like 'my little fat friend' started life as ad-libs in rehearsal and found their way artfully into various episodes sprinkling the show with a series of personal fingerprints by which we were instantly recognisable.

My 'short, fat, hairy legs' became a repeated jibe, the staccato slap on the face a ritual endearment. Those and the silly, end-of-show skipping routine, inspired by Johnny Ammonds after watching Groucho Marx, became gradual additions to a growing armoury of Morecambe and Wise trademarks which in public life could be two-edged.

I didn't mind when over-excited adults put on an impromptu version of our farewell dance, but I drew the line at being approached in a restaurant one by a cocky little lad who proceeded to slap me on both cheeks as Eric did in the show. I came very close to strangling the monster but managed, instead, a wan smile.

As long ago as the early Fifties we had been told by an Italian acrobat who was sharing a variety bill with us that we didn't work, we played. I have always taken that as a supreme compliment, knowing that we did work – and worked extremely hard at our routines – but that the final result appeared effortless, and the audience appeared merely to be eavesdropping on the two of us having a good time. The Morecambe and Wise Christmas shows were known in their heyday, when an audience of 26 million assured them a place in the record books, as the best Christmas parties at the BBC – hard work but great fun.

So, with Eddie Braben supplying us with material from his eyrie in Liverpool, with the two of us rested and in good health, and the BBC committed to providing us with full production back-up, Eric and I embarked on an eight-year period of sustained creative activity producing what we considered to be some of the best work of our lives.

8

Licensed to Amuse

Eddie Braben's writing routine was economy itself. On Monday morning a few sheets of paper would arrive in an envelope bearing a Liverpool postmark. There would be four or five gags on them, perhaps a couple of one-liners, and embryonic ideas for full-length sketches. We selected what we knew instinctively would work and rehearsed it in detail during the day, returning other sections to Liverpool for Eddie to rewrite. On the material we sent back we might also add ideas of our own for him to incorporate into the final product. Many a note began, 'Wouldn't it be a good idea if ...?'

The method was significantly different from Sid and Dick's. For one thing Eddie was never present at rehearsal. He preferred it that way, never setting foot outside his Merseyside fortress until the show was ready for recording. The three of us were in constant contact with each other at every step of the process, and even in the course of a day we could call him to rework a scene. On those occasions he would listen to our suggestions, go away for an hour or two and then phone down again with alterations or new jokes, which secretaries took down in shorthand, typed up and handed to us.

Later in the day we might get a visit from our musical director and choreographer, who in their turn would work on transforming the ideas into song-and-dance routines. The big thing was to try out the ideas as soon as possible. We could spend hours round a table theorising about a line, or simply howling with laughter at a gag, but unless we got up and acted it out we had no way of knowing if things would really come alive. Often what was funny in discussion failed to come off in practice, and what had looked flat and unpromising on the page soared once situation and character had been breathed into it.

We had now realised that the ideal duration of the show was forty-five minutes – that perfect compromise between the half hour that left an audience wanting more and the full hour that could take our routine into the area of diminishing returns.

The shows also benefited from being performed in front of a live audience. Big musical numbers, of course, had been recorded in advance and were projected onto an overhead monitor, but the back-chat and some of the sketches were performed, as they had been over most of our career, in front of genuine, flesh-and-blood members of the public who weren't forced to laugh if they didn't feel so inclined.

This, after all, was the way we had always performed so why sacrifice it for a canned laughter machine? Doing things live, though, could be dangerous. In the course of one scene, for example, taking place supposedly in our penthouse flat, we heard peculiar noises off but decided to pay them no attention. They began to get louder and clearly emanated from a carpenter or an engineer who had forgotten we were recording the show and who was busy making last-minute adjustments to the set. Not content with merely making a noise, he decided to put in an appearance as well, his ghostly outline moving clumsily across the rear of the set.

Remarking the presence, albeit in silhouette, of an unexpected participant in the sketch, Eric turned to the audience and said, 'He must have long legs. We're on the 13th floor!' At a stroke he saved the scene.

The recording of the show was the only time Eddie felt inclined to come down to London and the only opportunity he took to watch his disembodied gags take on an independent life of their own.

We introduced him to the audience as the man responsible

144

for writing the show and, after a short comic routine from one of our warm-up men – usually writers themselves, like Barry Cryer or John Junkin – we got into the show proper. Once it was over Eddie was back on a train to Liverpool ready to start scripting the next programme.

Peter Cushing initiated our long-running celebrity line-up and ensured himself a regular spot on subsequent shows by turning up as the disgruntled actor we had failed to pay. Even in real life people used to ask us if we had finally sent him the cheque. I doubt if they really believed we hadn't, but the shared lunacy of the very idea was a clear indication to us that we were getting the format right.

If the scene was going to succeed, however, we all had to work at it and, as a result, we insisted that anyone who agreed to come on the show had to rehearse with us for a couple of days.

And by that we really meant anyone. From Tom Jones to Elton John, from Harold Wilson to Vera Lynn, from Cliff Richard to Rudolf Nureyev. The rehearsal became all the more important the bigger the star.

We insisted, too (for their sake as much as for ours) that they came along to our rehearsal rooms to run through the script. It wouldn't work, we felt, if we went through a routine with Shirley Bassey, for example, at her suite at the Dorchester, as she had suggested. So they had to come to us, to very scruffy premises in Dalgarno Way behind Wormwood Scrubs Prison.

Rehearsals began at ten sharp and ran through to five with a short break for lunch of a very basic soup-and-sandwiches kind. It was an arrangement which didn't suit one of our earliest guests, the actor Robert Morley. Fond of his food and, dare I say it, a well-upholstered man to prove it, he was surprised at our spartan conditions and promised to put things right next day.

'Forget about the sandwiches tomorrow, dear boy,' he said to me. 'I'll take care of lunch.'

He arrived the next day empty-handed leaving us to assume that he had forgotten his promise.

Not so. At one o'clock a chauffeur-driven Rolls Royce arrived outside our rooms and the uniformed driver came in laden with six lunch boxes specially ordered that day from Fortnum and Mason. Bottles of wine accompanied this gourmet surprise in a gesture of lavishness not repeated by subsequent guests.

Indeed, the very opposite impression was conveyed by the actress Vanessa Redgrave, who turned up in baggy sweaters and jeans of such scruffiness as to make even our rehearsal clothes seem stylish.

She had the effortless talent, however, for totally transforming herself for the camera. From the rather down-at-heel individual she seemed at rehearsal she became the epitome of grace and elegance on stage. The contrast was very much part of the complex and contradictory personality which on one famous occasion got her physically ejected from the BBC's premises.

On that particular day she was booked for rehearsal and surprised us all by turning up armed with a handful of political leaflets which she began handing out to the staff. When asked to stop she refused and was promptly escorted away. The show eventually went well, but that day we felt she looked more at home on a picket line than in showbusiness.

*

Not all those we asked to appear with us agreed, of course. Sir John Gielgud turned us down, as did Michael Caine. Michael was concentrating on more serious roles at the time and felt that an outing with us wouldn't be appropriate, whereas Sir John, who maintained that he was a great fan of ours, gave no reason for turning down an appearance that could have made his name for him! He was probably not encouraged by my forthright approach to him in the BBC canteen where I inadvertently referred to him as 'Mr' Gielgud.

His fellow actor and knight Ralph Richardson initially turned us down but eventually agreed, only to discover that it wasn't at all what he had imagined. I went round to see him before rehearsals got under way, and it was clear that he wasn't a regular follower of the series. His wife was a great fan and had to explain to him what our humour was all about.

He was completely baffled by all this talk of 'can't see the join' or 'plays wot I wrote' and he seriously believed that the plays themselves were meant to be of Chekhovian subtlety. Not realising that they were meant to be vehicles for a series of broad gags, he insisted that he should get a decent playwright to create something for us.

'Couldn't we get Harold Pinter, or Arnold Wesker?' he asked in all innocence, while his wife stood by him vainly trying to make him see the point.

Although the sketch was very successful he never did see the point, and he spent half the rehearsal asking us why this or that was funny. After the show he continued in the same style, at a loss to understand what everybody had been laughing about. He ended the programme a very confused man. In fact, when it was all over, he said to his co-star, the actor Ian Ogilvy, 'I feel like a tom cat who's been left out all night on the tiles.'

From the same top drawer of the acting profession we also secured the services of Laurence Olivier, who at first was very hard to persuade. He agreed on condition that we film him at his home and use him only as a visual gag with very little dialogue. The idea, which was highly entertaining, involved him in repeatedly turning down my requests for him to appear on the show. That an actor of his standing should consent to deliver such devastatingly un-Shakespearian lines as 'Velly solly. Long number. Chinese raundery here' is a measure of the pull the shows had.

*

We worked very carefully with our guests, gently sending them up but strangely conspiring to be the butt of the jokes ourselves. My persona, for instance, of third-rate but self-important dramatist unaware of his own limitations was the perfect foil for Eric's down-to-earth brashness. And between the two of us we could provide an idiotic framework within which the star could be laughed at without being made fun of.

When Yehudi Menuhin came to see me at my penthouse flat, for example, he was told not to perform anything too elaborate – 'Just a couple of tunes on your banjo will do.' Rudolf Nureyev was told he was a last-minute replacement – 'We couldn't get Lionel Blair.' Our irreverence merely increased their status.

The lack of malice in the scripts and our golden rule never to make idiots of our guests meant that they could enjoy themselves and have nothing to fear. It also meant that even those doing the serious job of, say, reading the news could come onto the show, go through a routine and return to the job with dignity intact. How else could we have persuaded Angela Rippon to go through a high-kicking dance number when apparently delivering an important newsflash?

How else could we have persuaded the Prime Minister of the day, Harold Wilson, to meet us at our 'flat' (decked out with 'Vote Conservative' posters) and discuss the possibility of a starring role in a play of my own mad-cap invention?

'Don't give me any long conversations, lads,' he told us. 'Keep it short. You can do all the talking'. I have often wondered whether he thought that appearing with us was a vote catcher. After all we were very big then and a huge audience was guaranteed to any of our guests. He, too, was not disinclined to court the medium of television, and had a shrewd idea of what amounted to good publicity.

So it was that, come the transmission, he came on screen with his familiar trademarks, the pipe and the Gannex raincoat, to the total surprise and delight of our audience who had not expected that our drawing power might extend to one of the leading political figures of the day.

We always gave our guests copies of the script in advance but told them not to learn it. For actors this usually went against the grain of their experience, but it was vital to our own way of working. The script was merely a rough guide to the finished product and the precise dialogue would emerge only after the ad-libs and the re-writes had completely altered the first version.

Curiously enough, many actors found it very difficult to appear as themselves. This they were usually required to do in the first half of the show, turning up at the flat for a discussion of the text of 'the play wot I wrote'. Then, in the second half, they appeared in the 'play' itself which was the vehicle for most of the comedy and the element that the audience remembered most clearly.

The conflict between playing themselves and playing a part was most dramatically demonstrated to us by the actor Frank Finlay. We had put together an elaborate Casanova sketch which brought out Frank's acting talent superbly. He put on a tremendous performance both in rehearsal and on the night, injecting the part with a seriousness he would have brought to any mainstream theatrical production, but in the first half, as himself, he was catatonically insecure. He hated having to come on and play himself – so much so that while we were doing the scene in front of an audience he whispered to me, 'Come on, boys, I've had enough. Get me off now, will you?' and we were forced to shorten the routine in order to put him out of his misery.

Albert Finney was the same. Something inside him reacted strongly to playing himself in one of our sketches, and, as a result, he politely turned us down.

We had a bit of bad luck with the actress Sarah Miles, who was the only guest to accept and be forced to withdraw at the last minute. We had a sort of South Sea Island routine worked out for her, and at a meeting in a local restaurant – at which, incidentally, she wore the shortest mini-skirt I have ever seen – she was enthusiastic. It came as a shock to hear that she intended to pull out, and we could only assume that her husband, the playwright Robert Bolt, had taken one look at the play 'wot I had written' and advised her on no account to appear in such a suicidal production.

*

The thing I liked about trained actors was that they were good at improvising but, at the same time, very positive about learning their lines. They were disciplined enough to take whatever we threw at them, to take seriously whatever crazy sketch came their way and to put into it the care and attention they would have brought to any other stage or film part. And that was the real secret of the success of the sketches. However daft the ideas were, whatever lunacy the sketches demanded, the actors played things straight. Rehearsals were fun; performances were work.

Take John Mills, for instance, who appeared with us in a sketch set in a German prison camp where the inmates were plotting a bold but ludicrous escape involving the fabrication of a life-size dummy made to represent me. It was a spoof of the popular film 'Albert RN' where dummies were made to take the place of prisoners who, in the meantime, were tunnelling out of the camp.

We started off by giving Sir John a lot of the comedy lines but, as things progressed, he passed them all back to us because he wasn't sure he wanted the responsibility of the gag. He preferred playing his part straight and letting us have the tag line. Even so, as I remember, we did persuade him to wear a moustache and a kilt, so he must have had a finely tuned sense of the ridiculous.

The actor Ian Carmichael was less biddable. He was quite a prickly fellow to work with, a great professional but not easily slotted into the kind of comedy we embodied. But perhaps he had good reason for this approach since it occurs to me now that we involved him in a sketch with the most terrible tag-line, totally at variance with the urbanely surreal P.G. Wodehouse style of comedy which he performed so well. We had evolved a Dracula sketch for him which culminated in our

150

confronting the body of the sleeping Count lying in its coffin.

'Quickly,' said Ian, 'We must drive a stake through his heart. Has anyone got a stake?'

To which Eric replied, 'No, but I've got a couple of lamb chops.'

A terrible tag!

We had to treat both rehearsal and performance seriously, because there was so much time and money invested in them. Tying up studios for a couple of days shooting cost tens of thousands of pounds, and if we weren't thoroughly rehearsed we would waste hours and hours and pounds and pounds.

Props, too, had to be made well in advance – ten-foot-high ventriloquists' dummies, Egyptian settings, duck suits, Busby Berkley-style staircases, anything and everything. Such complicated gadgetry couldn't be left to chance. Building a prop fixed a joke for good. We could mess around with the lines, ad-lib and restructure as much as we liked, but once we had a physical prop on stage we had to use it in a very precise way – or throw it away altogether.

It was a costly business which relied on thorough preparation. And props aside, the preparation sometimes went against the grain. Persuading Robert Morley to sing, for example, was an uphill struggle, only equalled by our attempts to teach the actor Donald Sinden to dance.

*

In some ways Eric's heart attack and the weakened condition it left him in were to our advantage. Eric often admitted it himself. Had it not been for his state of health, we would probably have been following our crazy performing pattern of old up and down the country even then. As things were, apart from the occasional bank raid, we were forced to concentrate all our attention on television in a way that ensured high quality at every step of the production process. If we had been tearing about from theatre to theatre we could never have achieved the quality of those TV programmes.

151

The culmination of that work was usually on view in our Christmas Show, an event which seems to have had as cherished a place in the seasonal schedules as the Queen's message to the country and the Commonwealth. And if the Duke of Edinburgh's remark about the importance of the shows in the Royal Household is no exaggeration, we seem to have had as big a place in their festive routine as they had in ours.

Any good material we had not used in the year was usually saved for inclusion at Christmas. In addition, if we thought of a particularly good sketch which would be appropriate we shot it and stored it for later use. The Christmas programmes allowed us a five-week rehearsal period and the opportunity to go for big production numbers and big names.

*

Among those big names perhaps André Previn, Glenda Jackson and Shirley Bassey stand out most memorably in the public's mind. Largely, I think, because of the quality of the comic situation we put them in: André Previn as the conductor of a symphony orchestra performing Grieg's Piano Concerto with Eric as the bungling soloist; Glenda Jackson as a voluptuous Cleopatra surrounded by numbskull courtiers; Shirley Bassey singing 'Smoke Gets in your Eyes' while wearing a full length evening gown and size-10 army boots.

It was the uncluttered simplicity of the idea coupled with an economy and seriousness of execution which lifted those sketches out of the ordinary and into the realms of classic comedy. And it was all a team effort.

In the case of André Previn we were initially very concerned. He had agreed to do the show but, at the last minute, told us he had to be in LA for a concert and didn't expect to be back until the day of the run through. LA not being Luton Airport as we had thought, we were convinced he wouldn't have the time (or the stamina) to get to America and back for rehearsal.

A lot was riding on this sketch and we were genuinely worried – as was our producer. When the big day arrived Previn turned up right on time and word-perfect. We were amazed.

'How did you manage to learn the script so quickly?' we asked him.

'Oh, I just read it this morning by torchlight as I was coming in from the airport by taxi,' he said casually.

What would have taken Eric and me weeks to learn by heart he had learnt in a taxi ride. Our admiration was balanced only by our relief. We had a full symphony orchestra booked – each musician with his meter running – and delay or imprecision would cost a depressing amount of money and ruin a high-calibre routine.

His delivery was perfect and, as you would expect of a musician of his standing, his timing was razor-edged. Eric, as soloist, goes into his routine. Three bars later he is interrupted and reprimanded for playing (badly) something other than Grieg's Piano Concerto. The controlled impatience and the suppressed fury André Previn brought to that part was the work of as brilliant an actor as he was a musician.

'That's not Grieg's Piano Concerto. Those are not the right notes!' he says, prompting Eric to utter the classic line in absurdly logical defiance.

'They are the right notes. They may not be in the right order.'

The humour of the pay-off (which had even the orchestra in stitches) depended as much on André Previn's set-up as on Eric's delivery, and when the two worked, as they did perfectly on this occasion, the result was transcendant, delicious, incandescent comedy.

The point, too, was that no one lost face and André Previn (to Eric, 'Mr Preview') emerged from the experience, if anything, with his status increased.

*

153

Humour can be cruel. It needs a victim. The beauty of our routines was that we directed the cruelty on ourselves and both of us, Eric every bit as much as I, were the willing victims. No one appearing with us was ridiculed. It was this decision to deflect all the ridicule on to ourselves which made our comedy gentle. Nothing ruins a joke so completely as an attempt to explain it but, insofar as our comedy could be analysed, it was, I think, kind. Kind and innocent. We were given a licence to perform by a public who knew we would keep our comedy within acceptable bounds and who trusted us. We were not dangerous.

We sometimes performed our sketches in the flat, for example, in a double bed. And it was a measure of the innocence we projected that we didn't get complaints. At the time, someone in production suggested we use two single beds, but we refused. Many a time in our early touring days we had been forced to sleep in a double bed (lots of other performers did, too) but no one batted an eyelid. Admittedly it might seem rather quaint and old-fashioned nowadays, with a Laurel and Hardy feel about it, but in the late Sixties and Seventies we were able to get away with it without exciting any surprise or outrage, so innocent was our comedy.

On the rare occasion that a man and woman did find themselves in bed together it was quite clear to an audience that no 'funny business' was taking place – only funny business. In a scene with Diana Rigg, for example, who had been dressed to look like Nell Gwynne but who felt she looked like Danny La Rue, the joke involved the bed folding up into the wall with both of us on it.

'What have you been doing today?' asked my wife when I got home from filming.

'Going up and down in bed with Diana Rigg.'

Doreen carried on with her knitting unconcerned and unthreatened!

All this analysis apart, one simple fact remains. The comedy worked. And knowing that it worked, actors, actresses, musicians and others were attracted to us as a showcase for their own talents.

Glenda Jackson was the perfect example. Before she appeared with us she had earned a reputation as a fine actress in tough and controversial parts, such as 'Elizabeth R', 'The Music Lovers' and 'Women in Love'. That she might be good at comedy did not occur to many of her admirers who saw her more naturally in straight, rather 'heavy' roles. After she took part in the Cleopatra routine with us it was clear that her acting range was wider than many had been willing to believe. She was one of our most successful and frequent guests and, indeed, it was directly as a result of seeing her take to a comedy role so easily that she was selected to play opposite George Segal in the American film comedy 'A Touch of Class'.

In the same way, Dame Flora Robson, who had befriended us all those years ago in digs in Manchester, was delighted to be invited onto the show and to be given the chance to prove that she wasn't pining away in retirement or, worse, dead.

*

Our licence to amuse wasn't unconditional. It came with a couple of exclusion clauses. We would dearly have loved to have Prince Charles or Princess Anne as guests, but word came, via circuitous diplomatic channels, that they weren't available for work. Not even the promise of tea and sandwiches behind Wormwood Scrubs would induce them.

We sailed close to the wind with the Princess Royal, however, by incorporating her double in a sketch in the flat. Eric picked up the phone to 'have a quick word with the Palace' and soon afterwards a young actress with an astonishing resemblance to the Princess made her entry. We intended to use it as a trailer promoting a forthcoming programme, but somehow the press got hold of it beforehand and made a big fuss of it in the papers.

At about the same time we had a slight brush with the unions. It should have been a huge brush because we had booked half a dozen top trade union leaders of the day for an army sketch which involved a firing squad at dawn. But just as we were lining up the likes of Clive Jenkins, Jack Jones and Tom Jackson one of the actors enquired if they were Equity members, which they weren't. After vague threats about not working with non-union staff (and doubtless after the union bosses had figured what sort of a newspaper story this would make if it got out) the sketch was abandoned. Where were you, Vanessa Redgrave, when we needed you?

We also tried to use comparative unknowns throughout the series, people we had met in variety long ago who were willing to put in brief appearances as running jokes. Arthur Tolcher, for example, the harmonica player we had first met in Swansea in 1939, had a regular spot as a hyper-enthusiastic performer who had been promised a rousing finale but who had to settle for perennial disappointment when, each week, time ran out on him.

Another popular gag involved Janet Webb, a large and imposing lady who used to make an appearance at the end of the show. Up to that point nobody had seen her. She hadn't been in the show or even been mentioned. Then, at the last minute, she would sweep past us to the footlights and, curtseying and blowing kisses to the audience, would take all the credit for the programme with the line, 'Thank you for watching me and my little show. If you've enjoyed it then it's all been worthwhile so, until we meet again, goodnight and I love you all!' It was a clever ending which comically put us in our places lest people thought we had been putting the guests in theirs.

*

The reverse of that principle we used only rarely. And then only with the full co-operation of someone for whom our admiration was self-evident. Des O'Connor was perhaps the most popular of our rare sacrificial lambs. For the gag to work the audience had to know that we respected him professionally as a performer and liked him personally as a man – but that we had a mock rivalry that made us manic in our desire to get rid of him.

The sketch I remember best for this was one involving a long dramatic flight of stairs down which the three of us made our entrance – à la Fred Astaire – in top hat and tails. Unseen by the audience was a gap in the steps down which Des, without explanation, plunged into oblivion. We, meanwhile, continued our descent, a crazed gleam in our eyes. It was very effective and, for the thirty seconds or so that it lasted, extremely expensive.

One way of justifying the expense, of course, was to use the flight of stairs in another sketch, which is what we did with Penelope Keith. Again we appeared at the top of the stairs in wonderful, elegant outfits and slinked our way, equally elegantly, down to the bottom, only to discover that the last three steps were missing. The comedy came from our clumsy efforts to heave and manoeuvre the lovely Miss Keith onto the studio floor, and although the natural assumption would be that she was the butt of the joke the clear idiots in this caper were Eric and I. The guest, as usual, came out of it with dignity intact.

The only danger zone we noted involved guests who were comedians in their own right. And, to be honest, we rarely invited comics onto the show.

It's a fact as undeniable as it is self-evident that two comedians do not always hit it off. There is simply too much rivalry there for the relationship to flourish and, just as two opposites attract, two similar personalities tend to stay apart.

Perhaps that's the secret of my long personal friendship with Frankie Howerd who, for my money, is one of the leading comedians of all time. A classic English comic whose originality, verbal inventiveness and sense of subversive spontaneity put him in a class of his own. I am sure our friendship owes something to our different temperaments, so that whether playing tennis at his house in Malta or chatting over a drink at his cocktail parties we both bring something essentially different to the relationship. As Eric and I had done.

We had had an uncomfortable experience in the past and one which convinced us of the possible hazards encountered when one funny man comes face to face with another. It was very early on, when Sid and Dick were writing for us at ATV and when we had decided to invite Sammy Davis Jnr to appear with us. Long negotiations with agents and management and brushes with sturdily built minders at his London hotel suite had resulted in nothing.

We had a gap in the show which, at the last minute, Bruce Forsyth stepped in to fill. The trouble was that the combination of two forceful characters – Bruce and Eric – was potentially explosive. In the comedy routines we had at the time someone (usually the guest) had to take the submissive role as straight man and feed which Bruce was not temperamentally inclined to do. The result was two large egos metaphorically slugging it out on stage, each trying to top the other with an ad-lib or one-liner.

I don't know what it did to the audience but it frightened the living daylights out of me. Neither was willing to back down, the script was all over the place and the two of them held centre stage, each trying to bludgeon the other with comic repartee. I tried my best to bring the script back on course again and only partially succeeded. It was brilliant entertainment but a terrifying ordeal out there in front of an audience with mayhem all around.

True, we didn't expect our guests to behave with the flattering courtesy of The Beatles or Elton John, who insisted on calling me 'Sir' every time they asked for stage directions, but we did prefer them temporarily to submerge their comic tendencies in the interests of the script as rehearsed.

*

Did the fact that two comics together equal one comic too many mean that I was the stooge? I think not. And for a number of reasons. From the very earliest days Eric and I did two

different things which were never fundamentally in opposi-
tion. He was a comedian who danced and sang a bit; I was a
song-and-dance man who cracked jokes occasionally. Those
two sets of complementary talents fused over the years into an
act which gave us scope for both. Of course, most of the broad
comic lines went to Eric and most of the feeding was left to me,
but the act was always more than comic and feed. And
certainly, when we were doing our later work, Eddie Braben
created a comedy role for me which was independent of Eric's
ad-libs and back-chat.

I used to get rather tired of people saying, 'Of course,
Morecambe's the funny one.' And it could even be hurtful to
hear them add, 'He's so funny he doesn't need the other one.'
But remarks like that showed a basic misunderstanding of the
nature of a good double act. In a collaboration which broke all
the normal rules of mathematical logic *each* partner was more
than half the sum of the two. People who wondered 'What
would Wise have been without Morecambe?' were asking themselves the wrong question, because there was truly no answer
to that. What the act would have been without one of us –
whichever one – was simple. Not half so good.

The natural pecking order of our business meant that the
first name of the partnership tended to take star billing and
the second name was thought of as number two. But in our
case the convention didn't apply. And if some people thought
of me as someone in Eric's shadow because of his pre-eminent
comic role I was unconcerned.

Again for two reasons. The first: they were mistaken
because they had failed to grasp the essence of our comic
relationship. And secondly, as the comedian Ben Warris had
told me very early in my career, 'It doesn't matter who gets
the laughs as long as you get half the money.'

*

The higher we climbed, of course, the further we had to fall
and our very success induced a peculiar fear of its own – the
fear of failure.

We always conducted post mortems on the shows, first monitoring audience reaction, and then asking why this or that was not as funny as we had hoped. Sometimes there were simple technical reasons like sound engineers dwarfing a sketch with unduly loud sound effects which deadened the comedy, or the audience not being able to see some of the comic business from where they were seated.

Such defects were easily remedied. We merely moved the stage or gave the engineer a telling off. We found it very difficult to do comedy on the studio floor and so, true to our variety roots, we had a stage constructed directly opposite and slightly higher than the audience.

The stage itself was divided into three sections each prepared for a sketch. We might do the first sketch in the central stage, follow that with a film clip projected onto a monitor overhead and, while that was going on, prepare ourselves for the second sketch stage left. The idea was to have as continuous a show as possible to give things a spontaneous feel. This, meanwhile, was being recorded for transmission, suitably packaged and edited, the following week.

When the post mortem focussed on a non-technical hitch – a bad sketch, in other words – the difficulties were harder to iron out. There was no recrimination with Eddie. He, the producer, Eric and I blamed no one. We merely talked it through, offered observations here and there and mentally resolved to do better next time. It was too much to expect every show to be perfect.

A programme always had its low spots. But if ever a forty-five-minute show clocked up more low spots than high we were worried. The public will allow an entertainer to have one bad show provided it is followed by a good one. What they don't like is two bad shows on the run. Getting it right was a constant worry.

And getting it right was where the team-work came in. As soon as the script arrived we knew immediately what worked and what didn't. With the rest we sifted through to find the meat of the material and worked for hours on that. We might work all afternoon with only one funny line to show for it at the end. It was labour-intensive business.

Where we could help Eddie, our writer, and Johnny, our producer, was in being able to draw on over forty years of experience in variety. If Eddie wrote us a scene centred on a ventriloquist, for example, or an escapologist, we could call to mind all the acts we had seen (seen go wrong, as well) and incorporate them into the final gag.

We made something of a speciality out of bad vent acts. One involved a huge dummy whose head went off into the flies, and another involved Eric putting on a very large, fuzzy beard to prevent anyone seeing his lips move, both of them drawing on (and then exaggerating) music hall performers of old.

*

For many of our routines we were indebted to Bill King, the props man at the BBC. He could knock us up all sorts of gadgets from picture frames which fell off walls to Turkish slippers which curled suggestively when Eric kissed the girl. He made us a pair of alligator shoes, the toe cap of which opened up like a huge pair of jaws at the comic moment and devised, for a Mexican sketch, a set of maracas whose heads popped off, again suggestively, when something vaguely rude was going on in the background. It was a little naughty but still perfectly proper in the context.

Bill King's *pièce de résistance*, however, was the magnificent 'Singin' in the Rain' sequence, a water extravaganza of such elaborate inventiveness that he deserved an Oscar for it. The basic idea was simple – to do a spoof of the famous Gene Kelly number. To arrive at that point might take us five minutes of rehearsal time. The other seven hours and fifty-five minutes went into deciding *how* to do it.

And then, once we had decided that the bulk of the comic business would centre on Eric, as a New York cop, standing in the background getting wet in a variety of permutations, we

161

had to call on Bill to make the all-important set. Eventually, with valves and sluices and cisterns and conduits he created a wonderful three-dimensional construction which sprang surprise (but scrupulously timed) leaks at various points while I, in the foreground, went through the Gene Kelly song and dance.

The idea was sound, the props faultless and the execution perfect. So much so that at a gala dinner for Gene Kelly, the great man himself commented on it. He had done one of the classic song-and-dance routines in cinema history; we had done an equally classic comedy take-off. Neither could be bettered. It was a moment of great pride and satisfaction and, in the words of Janet Webb, if the audience loved it then it was all worthwhile.

*

By the mid-Seventies television work was accounting for most of our time. Bank raids became fewer and farther between. We did guest appearances, presentations, after-dinner speeches and so forth, but TV was what we now wanted to be known for. And we enjoyed the fame and confidence it gave us. The year 1977 was a year of decision.

We had worked for the BBC for eight years and our contract was up for renewal. Our policy had always been to sign for no more than 12 months at a time so as to retain our freedom. The arrangement with the BBC had been perfectly satisfactory, but in 1977 Philip Jones, head of Light Entertainment at Thames Television, offered us more money – something like three times what the BBC had been paying. To be leaving Bill Cotton was a matter of personal regret, but to be leaving the Corporation as such was a simple professional decision. Thames was offering a better deal so we accepted it.

There was talk at the time of disloyalty, which I think was unfair. The fact is that in our business it is wrong to talk in terms of loyalty. It simply isn't like that. If you produce the goods everybody wants you, and the minute you don't no one wants to know. It was inconceivable that managers would have been 'loyal' to us if we had ceased to deliver first-rate shows. And the same would have held true for every other performer.

The idea that the BBC or any other professional entertainment organisation would say, 'Well, so and so's not funny any more but he's a lovely fellah, so let's keep hiring him,' is ludicrous. Showbusiness is show-*business* and it's very tough. Like it or not, we were unique, and uniqueness sets its own price.

There is an old saying among pros, 'Be nice to people on your way up – you might need them on the way down.' That is an adage to which I have never subscribed because it is flawed. The fact is, when you are on your way down no one wants to know you at all. The advice Max Miller gave me in 1948 at the Town Hall, Watford was more reliable, 'Don't forget, boys, in this business when one door shuts, they all bloody shut!' From our early days before the war to when Eric died in 1984 our career was a constant progression through ever-opening doors for fear that, if we stood still for too long, one of them might just slam firmly in our face.

*

One opportunity which did not present itself to us and which, if it had, we would have grabbed with both hands was a situation comedy series of our own. In the TV shows we were only ever Eric and Ernie in the flat. We had no background, no situation, no relatives or friends to make more rounded characters of us. I always felt there could have been one step ahead, a move into a sit-com of the Hancock and James, 'Steptoe and Son', 'Only Fools and Horses' type. We occasionally received scripts but never any that showed real promise.

As the Seventies gave way to the Eighties we moved into a fifth decade of partnership. We had a solid body of work behind us and I, at least, was hoping for new horizons to explore. I still had the push, the ambition to keep going, the ultimate aim of getting to Hollywood.

It was an ambition Eric couldn't share. He had found another outlet for his talent, writing, and, with no previous training, had published a very successful first novel. He grew tired of doing the same variety routines, tired of the TV shows and tired, too, of being the funny man. The writing was giving him increasing satisfaction, and he once said he was prouder of his novel-writing achievement than he was of the comedy shows.

If he had lived longer I think it was inevitable that we would have worked together less – at least in the format of the Morecambe and Wise show. If he were still here today our friendship would have remained undimmed but our professional partnership would have been practically at an end. We would, of course, have done charity appearances and benefit concerts here and there, but our formal collaboration would have ceased.

At most we would have come together for one Christmas Show a year. I think both of us would have liked that and been happy to cope with the demands it would have made on us. But one show would have been enough.

The signs of his weariness with the Morecambe and Wise routine were clear enough. In the last year or so of his life he used to come to rehearsals drained of real enthusiasm, and even when it was time to record the show he had lost the drive to perform.

In the past, the time just before taking the stage had been one of great excitement. With the rehearsals behind us and the prospect of a great show in front of us we would relish the opportunity to go out there and perform. That after all was what we were good at: that after all was what we had devoted our lives to. Increasingly, though, in the last stages, Eric would turn up at the studio with no will to go on. He hated having to go through with it; he found it hard to go on.

Once he came into the dressing room and said, and I think I'm quoting him accurately, 'I'm not enjoying this any more.

164

I've had enough. I think I ought to stop it. What do you think I should do?'

'That,' I said, 'is something only you can decide.'

But decisions were not Eric's strong suit. In the early days he had had his mother to do the deciding; in later years I had seen to the arrangements. And there was another, more compelling reason why he could never have answered the question he himself had asked. He was a man of contradiction, and his lack of enthusiasm to perform was precisely matched by his compulsion to go on doing so all the time.

Wherever he went he performed. He was driven to it, and yet in his quiet moments later in life he hated it. If we were doing a personal appearance in some provincial town and we passed a wedding in progress, for example, he would make his way into the party and, to the delight of all the guests, get himself photographed with the bride and spend half an hour putting on an impromptu performance. When we received the Freedom of the City of London he couldn't resist that compulsion to entertain, to put on an ex-tempore show which entranced everyone who listened. The public loved him and he loved pleasing them.

One of Eric's great loves was fishing. This at least gave him the opportunity to put the business behind him and to unwind. But fishing was a relaxation only if he was alone. If there was anybody else on the riverbank relaxation was forgotten. One solitary fisherman sitting in a hollow by the water's edge became, to his own unexpected delight, an audience for Eric. Banter, gags, cross-talk and laughter filled the air, replacing the reflective calm Eric had come to the riverbank to enjoy in the first place.

He couldn't relax, couldn't be still and, although he hated the performing he was driven to do it all the same. It was that compulsion to entertain that took him to the Roses Theatre, Tewkesbury and to his very last appearance on stage.

Would he have given up if he had not had that fatal heart attack? I cannot be sure but I doubt it. I think he would have carried on, because not to carry on would have required a conscious, decisive move which that dear, dear man was happier to let others make on his behalf. If he hated performing he hated decisions even more, decisions which physical collapse after his last public performance took out of his hands for good.

*

The phone call came at the hour I dread, two in the morning. It had to be bad news, and it was. Joan, Eric's wife, gave me the details. Eric had been unwell, had come off stage early, had collapsed and been taken to hospital. He was dead and forty-six years of sharing had come to an abrupt and distressing end. I never saw him again.

Amid the confusion of those appalling moments of grief and pain I had a terrifying and unworthy thought. How could he do this to me? After all we had gone through together how could he abandon his partner?

9

Six Pennyworth of Wheezes

Two had become one. I was a solo act again. Eric had been robbed of the retirement he deserved and I had been robbed of a partner and a brother. After I had received the fatal telephone call I lay in bed thinking of all our time together, reviewing our joint professional career and reliving the countless moments of happiness we had shared.

I saw him again as the Flanagan and Allan impressionist, as the comedian with the dopey look when we first met as Bryan Michie discoveries. I saw the two of us starting out raw but determined to model ourselves on the great American double-acts, struggling on with very little money and perhaps a week's work at a time, and then slowly climbing the variety ladder and establishing a name for ourselves from Glasgow to Bournemouth. I relived our progression from second-spot comedians to radio and television performers; from the embarrassment of 'Running Wild' to the successes of the Morecambe and Wise shows. And what now?

At the funeral crowds of ordinary folk turned out in their thousands to mark a public farewell to a man who had brought so much laughter into their lives. The tribute show we performed later drew the same reaction from within the profession as all the big names of British light entertainment queued up to take part. But what now?

There were some half-hearted suggestions that I team up with other comedians in an attempt to put a double act together again. Some people had suggested I might work with

167

Bernie Winters who had been one half of a comedy team, Mike and Bernie Winters. Someone else even thought a collaboration with Eric Sykes might be fruitful. In that way, so the reasoning went, we could be 'Eric and Ernie' once more.

But it was foolish to think that we could. The magic had vanished forever and the public would not have accepted someone else – however good in his own right – as a replacement for Eric.

Nor, I think, would they have accepted me in any other new partnership. It was, quite simply, impossible to imagine anyone filling Eric's shoes. In forty-odd years of teamwork we had developed the sort of trust and understanding which could not be recreated overnight. An audience would inevitably compare the new hybrid act with the old one and it did not take a mindreader to conclude that the comparison would be unfavourable.

I decided to resist all suggestions of teaming up again so as to save myself embarrassment and the public disappointment. Even though we would have wished it otherwise, Eric's death had ensured that we went out in style, at the height of our popularity. Best to leave that memory unchallenged.

The immediate impact on my life was that, without an act, I had lost all clout in the profession. I had the respect and reputation but not the power to call the tune. Once the sympathy (which was very real and much appreciated by me) had worn off I was back among the hard realities of show*business*.

We all knew the score. I couldn't be expected to command the full production backing I had done before; I couldn't insist on appearing in shows. I had to wait to be asked. At the same time I was eager to work and impatient with any notion that the next stop was retirement. True to my Yorkshire upbringing I had saved wisely and put into practice the precepts of thrift my mother had tirelessly promoted. Financial worries did not beset me and, indeed, if I woke up at night fearful about the future (for Doreen's sake as much as for mine) I could at least be assured that a reasonable bank balance was a buttress against the worst of what life could throw at me.

But it wasn't enough. I needed the fulfilment which work brings and, although I was never manic about things, I felt that my life was my work and my work my life. And there was still a lot of life in me.

*

In 1985 I started working properly again on a show which was to take me right back to my roots as a song-and-dance man. It was exciting, challenging and more than a little nerve-racking.

I had been approached by an Australian agent named Lionel Abrahams, the mastermind behind my first solo appearance since Eric's death. He suggested a three-month tour of Australia working theatres, clubs and hotels. It was a welcome offer which I felt confident I could accept wholeheartedly. I began to work on an hour-long cabaret act, which would be flexible enough for me to extend if things were going well. And they did go well.

The Australians were a warm and friendly audience who constantly asked for the old songs and who could remember many of the old routines. Eric and I had been very popular down under, so I suppose I started off in credit. Even so, there was no disguising my apprehension backstage as I prepared to walk out as a lone entertainer for the first time in forty years. Once on stage, however, things were different. The nerves evaporated and I was at ease again, delighted simply to be there and gratified that my old touch had not vanished.

The new venture was overshadowed by the death, at the age of 85, of my mother. It added to the feeling of gentle regret which pervaded the atmosphere of the tour and meant, now that Eric had also gone, that I was on my own for good.

I opened with a medley of some of our old songs, 'Bring me Sunshine' and 'Following you Around', and went on with a couple of light gags and then into a dance routine. More songs followed, often of the Flanagan and Allan variety, after which I allowed time for requests from the audience.

I had a small orchestra behind me for backing and, all in all, a solid routine which took me from Perth to Adelaide and Sydney, enjoying a hearty reception wherever I performed. There was what I described as a nostalgia spot during which I projected slides onto a screen and talked about the old times in a casual way compiling, as it were, a visual autobiography. Then, at the end, came the time I left clear for questions from the audience. This was a very satisfying part of the act which enabled me to establish more of a rapport with the audience in a concert-party style.

Inevitably there was sadness at Eric's absence – I felt it as much as the audience did – but the tone of the evening was designed to be a gentle celebration of a life in showbusiness rather than a professional obituary: a mellow evening of song and dance and reminiscence.

The one thing the solo show got me out of was the 'who's best'. The 'who's best' is an old phrase for the curtain call which is, of course, supposed to be simply the moment when the cast comes down to the footlights to take a final bow. Inevitably, though, the moment acquires a less neutral significance when the performers come on to measure up against their fellow rivals.

The volume of laughter and applause is closely monitored as each artist makes that final entrance, the character and duration of the audience reception are mentally logged as each entertainer subtly eyes the others, wondering 'who's best' and secretly hoping it's him. The one-man cabaret relieved me of that.

*

I suppose I could have carried on with the act in Britain, touring it round the clubs and so on, but I felt it had come to the end of its natural life once I had returned home. I had introduced film clips of our shows in the odd television programme so, to some extent, there was no real need for that sort of act. A compilation programme with me filling in between comic excerpts fulfilled much the same purpose. I needed something new, and in 1987 one of the most rewarding, if sadly short-lived, episodes of my career began: a West End musical.

A big Broadway success at the time was 'The Mystery of Edwin Drood' – a stage adaptation of Charles Dickens's last, unfinished novel. It came complete with a clever theatrical trick – a choice of endings. Because Dickens had left the resolution of the plot up in the air it was open to the play's adaptors to devise one of their own. Their intriguing solution was to write in two possible endings which the audience, depending on their mood and inclination, would choose at will. It had won lots of Emmies in the States and seemed destined for similar success here.

When I was sent the script I was knocked out. I listened to the score and thought how wonderful it was. For the first time in a long time I was excited at the prospect of a brand new departure – to be offered a Broadway musical to start in London at the Savoy Theatre was something I had longed for.

As soon as I got the script I began learning it without delay, because I knew this was going to be one hell of a memory job. Sure, I had done musical numbers – Fred Astaire or Gene Kelly type dance routines – but only ever as one-off set pieces in the shows. This was of a wholly different order, involving page after page of dialogue and complicated music.

We had five weeks' rehearsal, but I had already begun three months earlier, such was my panic at the prospect of learning the lines. As it was, I turned up at the first rehearsal practically word-prefect, so than I was free to concentrate on what I did best – simply performing.

This wasn't the vehicle for ad-libbing. Actors and actresses – among them, Lulu – wouldn't have thanked me for making up the words as I went along. Messing about with some of the stage business, improvising a movement here or a gesture there was acceptable, but the text was out of bounds.

171

It was a new discipline for me. The part of the chairman, William Cartwright, was, I felt, tailor-made for me. We began with a fantastic opening chorus and settled into a pattern which had me either centre stage or seated to one side with a gavel keeping an eye on the proceedings. In some ways the rest of the cast looked to me as a focal point of the drama. I was the lynch-pin with the responsibility of moving the show on from sequence to sequence.

Only once did I fall victim to an attack of nerves. It was at the dress run when we performed the show from start to finish as if for real. We got into the musical number and I felt fine. Then we moved to my big speech, and half-way through I did the unthinkable: I dried. Drying during a song was impossible, since the music somehow always carried me through. Even if I were to become a little unsure I could kid it through and reach the end with no one really spotting that I had come adrift. But dialogue was different and there was no way of bluffing.

As I was half-way into the speech, alone and centre stage, my memory went blank. The silence that followed seemed to last an eternity and I prayed for the ground to open up beneath my feet and swallow me whole. I felt terrible. Terrible. Here I was in my first show, desperately wanting to make no mistakes and impress the cast and suddenly lost for words as they all looked on. It was a moment of anguish and embarrassment. Shortly afterwards I got back on course and we finished the dress run with no further hitches – much to my relief.

On the opening night the show went well, as it did for the whole of its brief life, and after my initial disaster I was never prey to nerves again. In fact the sheer weight of concentration made nerves impossible. For someone to whom line learning didn't come naturally the whole process was one gigantic, but equally delightful, effort.

We opened on a Saturday evening and I finished the show exhausted – more drained than I had ever been. I went to bed and didn't awake until Monday afternoon. As a sound sleeper

9. Six Pennyworth of Wheezes

at the worst of times I was amazed by such a marathon snooze. It was an indication of how much it had taken out of me. But the show made the effort worthwhile.

For all that, though, it wasn't judged a success. The critics didn't hammer the cast – so Lulu and I escaped unscathed – but they did put the boot into the music and the concept. As a result fewer and fewer people came to see it and we were playing to houses which weren't bringing in sufficient cash to keep it all afloat. With regret the producers announced to us that it was coming off after only a ten-week run.

We were all disappointed, of course, especially the younger actors and actresses who had hoped for extended employment in a hit show. I personally was disappointed when I thought of all the sweat I had gone through in preparing for my first crack at the 'legitimate' theatre. After the ten weeks I was beginning to get on top of the part and what I had had to concentrate so hard on was becoming more or less automatic. That left me free to give the performance that little bit extra, to inject into it a bit of me in order to make the role my own.

But just as I was moving into that phase where I could enjoy developing the character we were told that the show was coming off. And whereas for me it was a disappointment from the prestige point of view, for others it was a bread-and-butter disappointment which robbed them of a long spell of guaranteed income.

From where I was standing, though, despite the regret, I could reckon the whole episode a fantastic personal achievement. I had finally managed a full-length West End show from which I had emerged in one piece. I was getting a taste for this.

*

Before long I was being offered another part. This time by the impresario Ray Cooney, who runs the Theatre of Comedy and who was casting for the long-running hit 'Run for your Wife'. The theatre has a very good policy of changing the cast every

173

four months or so, partly to keep it fresh and partly to enable actors who are busy elsewhere to go off and do other things. A relatively short spell doesn't then tie the actors to a production which could lose them other work.

The play itself is foolproof and anybody with a sense of comedy and timing can slot into it to be guaranteed the laughs. My part was to be that of Det. Sgt. Porterhouse, a stock comic copper played at the time by Eric Sykes. I had been along to the show and watched how he had invested the part with a quite marvellous sense of subtle humour, but I had to be careful. I didn't dare to copy him, because what worked for him might not work for me. So I merely played it my own way, and the part fitted me comfortably enough to mould itself around me.

At this stage in my professional development parts really had to fit me. Producers knew what type of performer I was, what the influences on me had been, and what sort of stage role would suit me. Whereas young actors can take on new and unexpected parts and discover new and unexpected aspects of themselves to incorporate into the part, my persona, shaped by the twists and turns of long experience, was more or less fixed.

I was, as it were, an off-the-peg entertainer capable of being selected by imaginative producers and directors and being inserted ready-made into a production they thought suitable. I soon discovered something of a dilemma. What some people thought suitable didn't always suit me.

There were no end of offers of pantomime, for example, but here there was a problem. I had only ever done pantomime with Eric, as a self-contained act within a larger production. Now I was being offered parts like Baron Hardup or the Mayor, which were essentially straight feeding parts, and whereas it was one thing to feed Eric, with whom I had jointly made my name, it was quite another just to act as a straight man to someone else. Professional pride, you might call it, but it was an important consideration.

And still on the subject of pride, there were other things

which came into the equation. Which dressing room would I have? It may seem a trivial thing for those outside the profession, but for those inside it the pecking order is very important.

I was used to being number one, you see, and my position is very important to me. I was given the courtesy of the number one dressing room in 'Run for your Wife' even though technically it should have gone to the lead actor. My appearance on the playbill as a sort of guest star persuaded them to give me a touch of the VIP treatment, which I appreciated. I did not relish the RIP treatment buried away somewhere in dressing-room one hundred and four, so I turned down a number of offers which didn't seem to give me the status I felt I deserved.

In principle, though, there was nothing new about this attitude. It is very common among entertainers who, after all, live by their egos. I remember a long time ago in Coventry where Eric and I were playing the New Theatre with Harry Secombe in 'Puss in Boots'. Incidentally, the actress playing the feline part of the title was Gillian Lynne, who must have learnt a lot from the role as she went on to do the hit show 'Cats'. But I digress. Pecking order is what I'm talking about.

We were playing in 'Puss in Boots' for a rather pompous producer. He was responsible for putting on hugely successful spring and autumn shows with star-studded casts. On this particular occasion Eric and I felt that our billing was rather low down, so we asked him to change it. In reply we got a stiff letter to the effect that there were no stars in his shows and everybody was equal. To which we replied, 'Well, if we're all equal you won't object to putting our names at the top of the bill.' Like the 'who's best', billing is very important.

Perhaps it was rather grand of me, but it was also in a sense inevitable. Having been treated as the best it was hard to accept second-best in shows which, after all, I had been doing all my life anyway. For something different, something new and more challenging than straightforward pantomime I would have viewed things in another way entirely.

The same applied to the touring conditions. I have had

enough spartan digs and ropey dressing rooms to last me a lifetime. And at my time of life a four-week season as Mother Goose in a winter run on Tyneside held only marginal attractions.

Indeed it called to mind the story of the theatre manager who, in a pantomime performance of questionable authenticity, discovered some minutes before curtain-up that a comedian booked to play Mother Goose had dropped down dead in his dressing room. The cast was thrown into panic as there was no understudy to replace him. In desperation the manager took the stage and announced solemnly that there would be a change to the evening's entertainment because Mother Goose was dead.

'Oh, no, she isn't!' shouted the children as one.

In view of the less than full-scale respect a pantomime audience can bestow on performers (however elevated), perhaps my professional pride was understandable. The last thing I would want an audience (let alone a cast) to think is something along the lines of: 'Oh, what a shame. What's he doing that for? They were so good together and look at him now.'

So there is the dilemma again. I want to entertain but my position forces me to be careful about the roles I can accept. The dancing and performing have kept me in reasonable health, a state I try to maintain by swimming most days in the summer. In fifty-five years I have never missed a show, so there is life enough in me yet. I am as keen on this business today as I ever was and I am convinced I shall continue to be so. In short I want to go on working even though I have no material need to.

So is this drive to go on an unhealthy compulsion? I think not. Rather it is a perfectly understandable desire to do what I have been doing for as long as I can remember.

There are limits, as I have said, to what I would be prepared to do. Some shows wouldn't be worth the effort and discomfort of late nights and touring, of squalid dressing rooms and the thought of emerging into a rainy West End street to paddle

176

through rubbish inches thick and get home late and exhausted. But some shows would be worth it. The dilemma rests in deciding which. But if the right work is there, I am happy to go for it. After all, I'm still on my way to Hollywood and the perfect script may be just around the corner.

And another thing – I have an agent to support! The indefatigable Billy Marsh, doyen of them all, a man who engineered our move out of the bygone era of variety and into the medium of television, and a man who without complaint has kept a sure hand on the tiller when the seas have occasionally been rough. Well do I remember the mute frustration on his face when, a long time ago, Eric and I opened a jeweller's shop and were given a watch each as an appearance fee.

'How do I get my commission on this, boys?' he asked with pathos written in capital letters along the furrows of his forehead.

'Don't worry, Billy,' I said. 'I'll phone you twice a month with the time.'

The thing is, I'm not happy out of showbiz. I enjoy the company of pros, enjoy talking to them, swapping stories, reliving old times.

But not just the company of the old crowd: the new, up-and-coming generation, too. I like hearing their experiences and even, as something of an elder statesman of the entertainment field, giving them the benefit of mine. So I *do* miss the creativity of the shows Eric and I did. I *do* miss the sound of the orchestra behind me and the prospect of a big musical number in front. And I *do* miss the prospect of bringing all my energy and enthusiasm into a good show. When you know you have got a good show, and that you have done it well, there is nothing to equal the satisfaction, the buzz, the thrill.

But there are other compensations. There are appearances on TV in panel games and chat shows. It's easy to think that these are a come-down from the big-time, but not so.

You see, I have no hobbies. Or rather I have one hobby. It is

177

also my life and my work. Performing. So game shows and chat shows such as 'What's My Line' and 'Countdown' are my hobbies. They keep me and Doreen constantly in the company of the people we know, understand and love. What some of the engagements I accept may lack in creativity they make up for in conviviality.

Then, of course, there is the charity work, which can vary from recording a promotional record for the local council recreation department to raising money for a heart charity, Corda, by flying around the world in eighty hours dressed as Phileas Fogg. True, these were not performances demanding the highest level of creative energy, but they were entertaining to do and, in the end, profitable for the charities involved.

But all this activity, however varied, is linked by a common thread: the drive to keep on my feet in front of an audience. A man named Charles Henry, responsible for comedy productions at the London Palladium, summed it all up many years ago when he said to Eric and me in rehearsal that the only way to appeal to an audience is 'to go out there, give them six pennyworth of your best wheezes, and get off'. Whether in variety, in theatre, in public address, personal appearance or television I have followed that advice ever since.

*

So, please, if you have got this far don't snap shut the book and think, well, that's the last we shall see of him. Don't think, well, he had his day with Morecambe and Wise and that's the end of that. Even as you run your eyes to the end of what might (just might) turn out to be an interim autobiography, remember that I might be opening up a letter bearing an American postmark or taking a phone-call from several time-zones away in anticipation of a summons across the Atlantic – like I did in 1985 when I recorded a show called 'Too Close for Comfort' in Los Angeles. So I nearly made it to Hollywood.

Remember, too, that if the summons doesn't come I shan't be weeping into my tea.

178

9. Six Pennyworth of Wheezes

To end where I began: fame and success are delightful, but provisional and dispensable. And I can prove it.

I was once invited to a reception in the City of London, to a glittering banquet at the Guildhall in the presence of Her Royal Highness Queen Beatrix of the Netherlands. Bad weather and solid traffic delayed us, so we arrived late. Those with pink tickets had been presented to the Queen and were now making their way into the banqueting hall. We had pink tickets but we were too late for the presentation. As we moved into the hall I noticed that I seemed to be the only theatrical there. Why, I asked the equerry, had I been invited? I secretly knew why, of course. A lifetime's service to the entertainment industry. A place in the history books of British comedy. Adored and respected wherever the Queen's English was spoken. Oh yes, I knew why all right, but it would be pleasant to hear it from somebody else. The equerry went away and after a while returned.

'The reason you have been invited,' he said, 'is because you are a famous English clog dancer.'

Though I said nothing at the time, there was an answer to that ...

Index

Abbot, Russ 16
Abbott and Costello 52, 55, 81, 85
Abrahams, Lionel 169
after-dinner speaking 12-13
Ammonds, Johnny 112, 140
Angmering-on-Sea, Sussex; Villa
    Daheim 49
Anne, HRH Princess Royal 155
Ardwick Hippodrome, Manchester
    116
Askey, Arthur 39, 45-6
Associated Television (ATV) 118-22
Australia 169-70

Ball, Bobby 16
'Band Waggon' (show) 39-41, 45
Barbados 138
Bard, Wilkie 96
Barker, Ronnie 16-17
Bartholomew, Eric *see* Morecambe,
    Eric
Bartholomew, Sadie (Morecambe's
    mother)
  and Morecambe's early career 48,
    104, 115, 165
  and Morecambe and Wise 52-3,
    53-4, 56, 57, 66, 73
  and 'Running Wild' flop 115
Bartlett, Joan *see*Morecambe, Joan
Bassey, Shirley 145, 152
Batley, West Yorkshire
  Jimmy Corrigan's Variety Club
    133-4
Beatles 158
Beatrix, Queen of the Netherlands
    179

Ben Reed (ship) 63
Berganjo Brothers and Juanita 94
Black, Alfred 110
Black, George 56-7, 57-8, 110
Blackpool 110-11, 113
Blythe, Doreen *see* Wise, Doreen
Bolt, Robert 149-50
Boswell, Eve, 111
Braben, Eddie 139-40, 141, 143,
    144-5, 159, 160-1
Bradford, West Yorkshire; 'Nignog
    Revue' 36-7, 38
Brighton; Grand Theatre 84
BBC *see* radio *and under* television
Brixton Empire 110

cabaret act, Wise's Australian
    169-70
Caine, Michael 146
Cannon and Ball 16
Cardiff 111
Carmichael, Ian 150-1
Carne, Roger 94
Carr, Pearl, 121
'Carson and Kid' 28
catch-phrases, Morecambe and
    Wise's 12, 140
Clapham Grand Theatre 79-83
Cleethorpes, Lincolnshire 33-4
clog dancing 28, 30, 40, 179
Cogan, Alma 114
Command Performances, Royal
    Variety 14, 122, 127
Compiegne (French liner) 61-2
concert party 70-2
Cooney, Ray 173

Corbett, Ronnie 16-17
Cotton, Bill 130, 137, 139, 162-3
Coventry; New Theatre 175
Cribbins, Bernard 14
Crosby, Bing 125
Crowther, Leslie 71
Cryer, Barry 145
Cushing, Peter 145

Davis, Sammy, Jnr 158
Dennis, Reggie 84
Dewsbury Empire Theatre 105
Dodd, Ken 139
Duer, Mrs (theatrical landlady) 66, 73, 76, 83

East Ardsley Secondary School, Leeds 34-5
Edinburgh, HRH Prince Philip, Duke of 130-1, 152
Edwards, Jimmy 98
Eliot, T.S. 85
Elizabeth, HRH Queen, the Queen Mother 131
Elton, Ben 15-16
Emery, Dick 13-14
Empire Theatres 89-90

films, Morecambe and Wise's 126-7
Finlay, Frank 149
Finney, Albert 149
Finsbury Park Empire 89-90
Firelighter, The (ship) 62-3
Flanagan, Maureen 43
Forsyth, Bruce 71, 122, 158
'Front Page Personalities' (show) 84-5

Gable, Clark 59
Gielgud, Sir John 146
Glasgow Empire 9, 98-9
Golders Green Hippodrome 105
Grade, Leslie 101
Grade, Lew, Baron Grade of Elstree 116, 128-9
Green, Sid 118-19, 120, 121, 130, 138, 143

Hall, Adelaide 53
Hancock, Tony 78, 163
Henlere, Herschel 100
Henry, Charles 178
Hicks, Bert, 54
Hills, Dick 118-19, 120, 121, 130, 138, 143
Hitchcock, Alfred 59
Holbeck, Leeds; club appearances 33
Hope, Bob 125
Horne, Lena 116
Howerd, Frankie 157-8
Hulme Hippodrome, Manchester 106
Hylton, Jack 39-41, 44-5, 47, 49, 56-7

Intelligence Men, The (film) 126

Jackson, Glenda 152, 155
Jackson, Tom 156
James, Jimmy 99
Jason, David 17
Jenkins, Clive 156
John, Elton 145, 158
Johnson, Lyndon B. (US President) 125
Johnson, Teddy, 121
Jones, Alan 110-11
Jones, Jack 156
Jones, Philip, 162
Jones, Tom 145
Jones, Smith and 17
Junkin, John 145

Kafka, Paul 140
Karas, Anton 101
Keith, Penelope 157
Kelly, Gene 162
Kerr, Deborah 59
Kilburn; Empire Theatre 83
King, Bill 161-2
'Knee-Deep in Daisies' (song) 29, 38-9, 40

Leeds
    Empire Theatre 89
    Wise's childhood in 20-39

Index

Wise returns during War 49-50
Leicester Opera House 105
'Let's Have a Tiddly at the Milk Bar' (song) 30, 39, 40
Linda and Lana 88
Little and Large 16
'Little Pal' (song) 30-1
Liverpool Empire 54, 89
London, Freedom of City of 165
London Palladium 122, 127-8
Lucken, Wally 67
Lulu 171, 173
Lupino-Lanes, the, 84
Lynn, Dame Vera 145
Lynne, Gillian 175

McKay, Mrs (theatrical landlady) 105-6
Magnificent Two, The (film) 126
Manchester 105-6, 116
Marsh, Billy 74, 117, 118, 177
Menuhin, Yehudi 148
Merchant Navy 61-6
Michie, Bryan 38, 39, 51, 53, 54, 64
Miles, Sarah 149-50
Miller, Max 100, 163
Mills, Sir John 150
Morecambe, Eric (Eric Bartholomew)
 early solo act 48-9, 167
 partnership with Wise *see under* Wise, Ernie
 war service in mines 61, 83-4
 marriage 108
 first heart attack 10, 19, 84, 126, 134-6, 151
 death 10, 19-20, 165-6
 character 18-19, 102, 119, 165-6; insecurity 18-19, 115, 124; limits of ambition 103, 104, 164
 dislikes USA 124
 family life 18, 19, 109, 126
 fishing 165
 love of performing 165
 mother's influence 48, 104, 115, 165

Morecambe, Joan (*née* Bartlett) 108, 166
'Morecambe and Wise Show, The' 9, 130, 143-62, 162-3, 167
Morley, Robert 145-6, 151
Moss Empires 89-90
'Mystery of Edwin Drood, The' (musical) 171-3

Navy, Merchant 61-6
Naylor, Mary 51-2
Nignog Revues 36-7, 38, 46
Nino and his Wonder Dog 94
Norval, Gordon 74, 79
Nottingham 73
 Empire Theatre 89
Nureyev, Rudolf 145, 148

O'Connor, Des 71, 98, 135, 156-7
Olivier, Laurence, Baron Olivier of Brighton 147
'Only Fools and Horses' (television series) 17, 163
Oxford; New Theatre 52

pantomime 101-2, 105, 174
Parnell, Val 99
Petite Poupée, La (trapeze act), 94
Petrov, Anton 68
'Piccadilly Palace' (show) 128
Pleon, Alex 58-9
Pope, Frank 74, 116
Potter, Maureen 43
Preston Guildhall 12
Previn, André 152-3
Prince of Wales Theatre, London, 57, 59
Princes Theatre, London 39-41

radio
 Wise's local broadcast as child 23, 39
 Morecambe and Wise on 59, 103, 111-12
Redgrave, Vanessa 146
Rice, Tim 14
Richard, Cliff 145

Richardson, Sir Ralph 146-7
Rigg, Diana 154
Rippon, Angela 148
Robeson, Paul 116
Robson, Dame Flora 106, 155
Rodway, Mrs (Hylton chaperone) 43, 44, 47
Royal Family 130-1, 152, 155
Royal Variety Command Performances 14, 122, 127
'Run for your Wife' (play) 173-4, 175
'Running Wild' (television series) 112, 113, 114-15, 167

Sanger, Lord John; Circus and Variety 66-73
Secombe, Harry 90, 175
Seddon, Mollie 67
Sheffield; Lyceum Theatre 105
Sinden, Donald 151
'Singin' in the Rain' sequence 161-2
Smith and Jones 17
Stewart, James 59
'Strike a New Note' (show) 57-9, 61
Sullivan, Ed 122, 125, 138
Swaffer, Hannan 95
Swansea
   pantomime 102
   'Youth Takes a Bow' 49, 51-2
Sykes, Eric 168, 174

Tattersall and Jerry (ventriloquist act) 93
Telegraph and Argus (newspaper, Bradford, West Yorks) 36-7, 38
television
   ATV series (1961) 118-22, 128-9
   BBC; 'Morecambe and Wise Christmas Shows' 130-1, 141, 152, 164; 'Morecambe and Wise Show' 9, 130, 143-62, 162-3, 167; 'Running Wild' 112, 113, 114-15, 167
   Thames TV 162-3
Tewkesbury; Roses Theatre 165, 166
Thames Television 162-3

That Riviera Touch (film) 126
Thorpe Junior School, Leeds 34
Timperley, Mr (of 'Nignog Revue') 37
Tolcher, Arthur 52, 156
'Two of a Kind' (song) 120, 121
Two Pirates, The (speciality act) 94

United States of America 122-5, 138

Vadden, Henry 92-3, 94
Van Damm, Vivian 76-8
Variety Club of Great Britain 127
'Variety fanfare' (radio programme) 111
Vogelwein's Bears 94

Waldman, Ronnie 114
Wales, Diana, Princess of 11
Walthamstow; Palace Theatre 75-6
Ward, Dorothy 36
Ward, Eddy 35-6
Warris, Ben 159
Watford Town Hall 100
Webb, Janet 156, 162
Williams, Cissy 90, 98
Wilson, Harold, Baron Wilson of Rievaulx 145, 148
Wilson, Keppel and Betty 94-5, 104
Windmill Theatre 76-8, 90
Windsor Castle 130-1
Winters, Bernie 168
Wise, Doreen (*née* Blythe)
   courtship 69-70, 84
   marriage, 108
   home life 18, 19, 109-10, 126, 154
Wise, Ernie (Ernest Wiseman)
   Early career
   childhood 21-6
   education 32, 34-5, 47-8
   early performing career in North 23, 27-38
   audition and move to London 38-41
   with Jack Hylton 39, 42-9
   changes name to Ernie Wise 45

meets Eric Morecambe 48-9, 167
returns home during War 49-51
in 'Youth Takes a Bow' 51-7
Partnership with Morecambe
early double act 18, 51, 52-9, 61
in Merchant Navy 59, 61-6; per-
    forming career continues
    during service 64-5
resumes partnership with
    Morecambe 66
with Lord John Sanger's Circus
    and Variety 66-73
theatrical work after Sanger's
    Circus 73-9
success at Clapham Grand
    Theatre 79-83
subsequent theatrical work
    83-111
marriage 108
1950s work in radio 111-12
entry into television 113-22
in USA 122-5
films 126-7
leaves ATV for BBC 128-9
and Morecambe's first heart
    attack 136, 137-9
'Morecambe and Wise Show', BBC
    TV 130, 139-41, 143-62
move from BBC to Thames Tele-
    vision 162-3
partnership nearing end 10, 19,
    163-6
style of partnership 17-19, 71, 72,
    85-8, 97-8, 104, 158-9, 168
Resumes solo career 167-79
Australian tour 169-70
theatrical work 171-5
Personal life and character
ambition 104, 163-4
health 127, 176

love of performing 10-11, 14-15,
    177-8
marriage 69-70, 84, 108; home life
    18, 19, 109-10, 126, 154
*see also individual songs and
    shows and*: radio; television
Wiseman, Ann (Wise's sister) 24
Wiseman, Arthur (Wise's brother)
    24
Wiseman, Connie (Wise's mother)
    21-2, 23, 168
and Wise's childhood performing
    career 32, 37-8
death 169
Wiseman, Constance (Wise's sister)
    24
Wiseman, Gordon (Wise's brother)
    24
Wiseman, Grandmother 26
Wiseman, Harry (Wise's father)
    21-4
performing career 24, 27-36, 38,
    41
and Wise's move to London 40-1,
    50
health 41, 27
death 130
Wonder Wheelers, The (speciality
    act) 94
'Woody Woodpecker's Song' 82-3
'Workers' Playtime' (radio show)
    103, 111
Worth, Harry 96, 110

Yelding, Speedy 67
'You're Only Young Once' (radio
    show) 111-12
'Youth Must Have its Fling' (radio
    show) 59
'Youth Takes a Bow' (revue) 49, 51-7